KU-357-615

The World's Classics

487

PLATO : SELECTIONS

Oxford University Press, Amen House, London E.C. 4

GLASGOW NEW YORK TORONTO MELBOURNE WELLINGTON

BOMBAY CALCUTTA MADRAS CAPE TOWN

Geoffrey Cumberlege, Publisher to the University

PLATO

SELECTED PASSAGES

Chosen and edited by

SIR R. W. LIVINGSTONE

President of Corpus Christi College
Oxford

Geoffrey Cumberlege

OXFORD UNIVERSITY PRESS

London New York Toronto

PLATO

Born at Athens, probably in 428 B.C.

Died 347 B.C.

The present volume of selections from the Dialogues of Plato was first published in 'The World's Classics' in 1940 and reprinted in 1941 (twice), 1945, and 1948.

Must do my Plato. I'm never well without that.

J. RUSKIN.

The Greek philosopher who laid the foundation of all our finer thoughts.

PROFESSOR A. N. WHITEHEAD.

Plato was my first and chief political teacher.

PRESIDENT MASARYK.

PRINTED IN GREAT BRITAIN
AT THE UNIVERSITY PRESS, OXFORD
BY CHARLES BATEY, PRINTER TO THE UNIVERSITY

CONTENTS

	Introduction	vii
I.	Socrates	1
II.	The Spiritual Life: Love	41
III.	Religion	76
IV.	Politics: Ideals and Realities	85
V.	Education	145
VI.	Moral Ideals	162
VII.	Art and Poetry	186
VIII.	Miscellaneous	193
IX.	Fables and Myths	204

INTRODUCTION

PERHAPS no thinker has had as deep and permanent an influence on European thought as Plato, and many people meet him there without recognizing him. He is present in some of the greatest English poets: if he had never lived, Spenser, Shelley, Coleridge, Wordsworth, Bridges, would not have written some of their most characteristic poetry. He is present in politics. 'The Communist party, like the Fascisti, owes its general conception to that germinal idea of the Modern State, the Guardians in Plato's *Republic*. If anyone is to be called the Father of the Modern State, it is Plato.'[1] He is present in religion; the opening sentences in St. John's Gospel reflect his thought, and he was the first to argue that 'the things which are seen are temporal, but the things which are not seen are eternal'.[2] The extracts that follow will show how living are his subjects and his thought. Almost every problem that he discusses is a modern problem.

Those who read him study at the same time a man, in a different way as great as Plato—Socrates, his master. The two thinkers are united by a relationship to which history has no parallel. Socrates wrote nothing and we should know hardly anything about him, if two men who heard him in their youth had not published

[1] H. G. Wells, *The Shape of Things to Come*, p. 139.
[2] 2 Cor. iv. 18.

accounts of his conversations. One of these men, Xenophon, first a soldier of fortune and later a country gentleman, had literary tastes but a mediocre mind.[1] Plato, the other, is one of the greatest thinkers and writers of the world. Yet none of his thirty odd 'Dialogues' profess to state his own views: the chief speaker in all except the later ones is Socrates; in none does Plato himself appear, and there are only two brief and incidental mentions of him. One might almost say that Socrates wrote nothing, and that Plato said nothing but was content to be the mouthpiece of his master. But though the voice is the voice of Socrates, it does not follow that the thoughts are his, and scholars have never agreed how far the ideas in the 'Dialogues' come from the master or the pupil.

Socrates, a man with thick lips, flat stumpy nose, eyes set widely apart, and so ugly that his friends compared him to a satyr, was the son of a working sculptor and a midwife, and born about 470 B.C. He led the life of an ordinary Athenian citizen, serving in the army and taking his share in politics, but spent most of his time in places of public resort discussing with anyone who would listen problems of religion, conduct, politics, education, or ordinary life, till at the age of 70 he was put to death on a charge of irreligion and corrupting the young.

He has two aspects. He is the chief saint and martyr of the ancient world—one of those men who see how life should be lived and live it

[1] Xenophon's *Memorabilia*, his chief account of Socrates, is translated in the Everyman Library.

accordingly, unswerving through all temptations and difficulties. But his intellectual importance is as great as his moral force. Unlike Plato, he had a philosophic method, but no philosophic system. His central doctrine was that goodness is knowledge, that if a man knows what is right he will do it, and that the secret of success in life is to have clear and true ideas about it. Hence his characteristic methods; his search for a general principle on which to base each action and thought; and his incessant questioning of people about the exact meaning of the words that they used. None of us in the presence of Socrates could have safely indulged in our normal practice of using words without a precise idea of their meaning. If Socrates was alive to-day, he would be asking our politicians, journalists, and others what exactly they meant by liberty or democracy or a classless society, or by any other slogan or catchword of the moment. It is the misfortune of every nation that Socrates is not alive and has left no successors.

But he was no mere barren critic. Behind these perpetual questions lie three positive principles, which might be phrased thus. Whatever you do, whether it is choosing a political creed, or a profession, or a husband or wife, think hard, much, and closely about it. Believe in truth and in the search for truth; and be confident that if men think strenuously and honestly, they will reach the right views not only about politics but about life itself. Above all, be intellectually humble, hold convictions firmly but not arrogantly, welcome criticism and try to learn from it, and if you criticize others, criticize yourself too.

In a sense Socrates made Plato, but he made something very different from himself. The two men are wholly unlike in personality, genius, origin, and life. Socrates came from the lower *bourgeoisie*, Plato belonged to one of the oldest families in Athens, and if we had met him in the closing years of the fifth century, we should have seen a brilliant young aristocrat, destined for a political career, discontented with the weaknesses of contemporary democracy, and with an idealistic hope of reforming it. At the same time he had many other interests; he had won the wrestling competition at the famous Isthmian games, he wrote tragedies now lost, and poems—among them two of the finest surviving Greek epigrams—he frequented the company of thinkers of the day, and, like all the intellectual young men of Athens, he was an associate of Socrates. In 404 B.C. at the age of 25 he seemed one of the coming statesmen of his time.

The following extract from one of his letters shows what transformed him from a politician into a philosopher.

'I thought that as soon as I became my own master I would immediately enter public life. A sudden change, however, in the political situation diverted me from my plan. The democratic régime of the time was generally detested and a revolution took place, headed by a supreme committee of thirty. Some of the members of this supreme committee were relations or acquaintances of mine and invited me to join them, imagining that I would find the new régime to my taste. My feelings were in no way surprising if you consider my age at the time. I thought that it would substitute the reign of justice for the reign of injustice, and so I gave it my closest attention to see what it would do. And I saw these gentlemen within a very short time make the democracy they had destroyed seem like a golden age! I was deeply disgusted and dissociated myself entirely from this deplorable government. Shortly afterwards, the Thirty were turned out and their régime destroyed. Once again I was filled with a desire to take an active part in politics. It was not surprising that those revolutionary times resulted in personal reprisals of a violent character: but on the whole the restored democracy exercised considerable moderation. And yet, as ill-luck would have it, certain influential persons brought an action against Socrates. The charge was an outrageous one, of which Socrates was completely innocent. They accused him of irreligion, and on this count the jury condemned him to death.

'When I considered all this, the type of men who were administering affairs, and the condition of the law and of public morality—the more I considered it and the older I grew, the more difficult appeared to me the task of decent government. Traditions of conduct and the actual observance of law alike were degenerating in Athens with surprising rapidity, and when I saw how chaotic the political situation was, I felt completely baffled. I continued to consider how some improvement could be brought about, not only in the administration, but also in society as a whole, and I was constantly on the look-out for an opportunity to intervene. But finally I came to the conclusion that every state without exception is badly governed, and that the state of legislation is everywhere so deplorable that no improvement is possible without drastic reconstruction combined with some very good luck. And so I was forced to extol true philosophy and to declare that through it alone can real justice both for the state and for the individual be discovered and enforced. Mankind (I said) will find no cessation from evil until either the real philosophers gain political control or else the politicians become by some miracle real philosophers.'[1]

These words make Plato's story clear. The young idealist found politics very different from his dreams. He had hoped to reform the democracy, but his own oligarchic friends proved worse than the régime which they replaced; and the democracy, when it recovered power, put to death the teacher of whom he says, 'of all the men of his time whom I have known he was the wisest, the most righteous and the best'. It seemed impossible to reform politics from within, and better to withdraw and in quiet study think out the principles on which a state could be created where men might lead the good life. So a man in modern Russia or Germany or Italy might feel: indeed Plato's experience must have closely resembled that of those Germans who, seeing the weaknesses of the Weimar Republic, turned to Nazism in hope of better things, only to find a worse disillusion.

The crisis which Plato had to face was much more than political, and it so closely resembles our own, both in its causes and its phenomena, as to be of special interest to us. In brief it

[1] *Letters*, vii. 324—tr. Crossman.

was the crisis of a civilization, whose traditional beliefs had been destroyed by scientific thought, and whose fabric had been still further shattered by a great war. We think of the late fifth century as the age when the ideal of democracy was conceived, and the greatest body of drama and some of the greatest art in history was created. But it was also an age of spiritual confusion and unrest. Intellectual criticism had begun by upsetting current beliefs about the universe, and then turning to religion, morals, and politics had been equally destructive there. Some of the extracts that follow show how acute, drastic, and disturbing it was.[1] On the top of this came a war which lasted nearly thirty years; and war, as the historian of the day says in words which this generation can well understand, 'is a savage teacher, which brings men's characters down to the level of their fortunes'.[2] This was the world into which Plato was born. Its civilization was shaken to its foundations. His work was to restore it. That fact gives a peculiar quality to his writing. He was a philosopher; but an essentially practical philosopher. To think of Plato as a theorist is wholly to misconceive him. He is not of the type of Descartes, Spinoza, Kant, or Hegel. At the age of 25 his interests were in politics, and in practical politics; they were the same when death found him with his last treatise, *The Laws*, incomplete. It is this practical interest which makes Plato so stimulating as a political thinker. We may disagree with his

[1] e.g. pp. 79, 162 ff.
[2] Thucydides, iii. 82.

views, but we cannot mistake his passionate desire to find the right life for man and to create a state in which it can be lived, and a reader must be very cold or very unintelligent who is not moved by his ardour.

After the death of Socrates he left Athens for eleven years, travelling in Greece, Sicily, and probably in Egypt and North Africa. In Sicily he made three interesting but unsuccessful interventions in practical politics, but most of his life was spent in the Academy at Athens, where he and his friends worked, and where he died in 347 B.C. at the age of 81, still working. The Academy was the name of the suburb where Plato bought a house and garden. He bequeathed it by will to be used for philosophical study, and in this way the word has acquired its modern meaning, for it became the first university of the world and had a longer life than any other; founded about 380 B.C., it was only closed in A.D. 529.

More than forty works are attributed to Plato, and of these some thirty are genuine. All, except the *Letters* and the speech of Socrates at his trial, are dialogues or conversations, in most of which Socrates is the chief speaker. Plato was more than 30 when the earliest was written; the last, the *Critias*, was unfinished when he died, but shows no failing of the writer's powers. He deals with many subjects—language, poetry, logic, the theory of knowledge, education—but his greatest writings are on religion, morals, and politics, for his deepest interest is life—how to live, the nature of man and what makes him happy, the human soul and its destiny and its place in the universe and on earth.[1] That takes him on to politics, for man can only live a full life in the state, and he can only live a good life in a good state.

Without knowing anything of his theories, every intelligent person can enjoy the best passages in Plato, and can see his literary art, his knowledge of human nature, and the power of raising fundamental problems which makes him so good an introduction to the study of ethics and politics. But under all the wealth and interest of his views on art and conduct and the world lies a consistent philosophy without which they cannot be fully appreciated and which is worth grasping, because it is the first statement of the claims of the spiritual life, and the most important contribution ever made to the philosophy of religion. Its centre is a doctrine, usually described by the unilluminating and unattractive title of the 'Theory of Ideas', which at first seems to have little to do with religion, for it begins with the problem of knowledge, though it develops into a theory of the world and of human life. The following is a sketch of it.[2]

1. How do we know? What is it that we know? Take for instance a chair. There are millions of different chairs, hundreds of different kinds of chairs. When we see a chair, we see a particular piece of wood or steel; but we call it a chair because we recognize that it belongs to a certain class of things with certain characteristics.

[1] See esp. the *Gorgias*, *Phaedo*, and *Republic*.
[2] Chiefly taken from the author's *Portrait of Socrates*.

The word used by Plato for 'class' in this sense is εἶδος, which has been turned into English as 'Idea'. But it has nothing to do with what we mean by that word. It means Form, and this word suggests better what was in Plato's mind. In modern philosophic language it would be called a 'Universal'. To this 'Idea' or 'Form' or 'Universal' of a chair all the particular chairs in the world are somehow related, and in virtue of this relation we call them chairs. So with every other concrete thing—tables, beds, houses, &c. Each of them has its 'Idea'. It is the same with abstract things like Beauty, Justice, &c. Behind each beautiful object is the 'Idea' of Beauty, in virtue of which we call it beautiful, behind each just action is the 'Idea' of Justice, in virtue of which we call it just. So, when we come across a chair or a just action, we only know it because we know the 'Idea' which lies behind it. We know 'Ideas', 'Forms', 'Universals', and we know particulars only through these.

2. How do we know 'Ideas'? Not through the senses; we can see or touch a chair, but not the 'Idea' of a chair. That is grasped not by the senses but by the mind. This is even more obviously true with Beauty, Justice, Courage, Truth: these are grasped by the mind.

3. So far we have been dealing with a theory of knowledge—one which for the most part would be commonly accepted to-day. But, in Plato's hands, this theory of knowledge becomes something much more important; it leads to conclusions which, if true, profoundly affect our view of life. The 'Idea' of a chair is more perfectly

a chair than any concrete chair. The 'Idea' of Beauty is more completely Beauty than any beautiful sight or person. But if the 'Ideas' are more perfect than any particulars, they are more important. Their world is the real world, beside which the world of our senses is a shadow.

4. So we get a conception of two worlds, the higher world of the 'Ideas', supra-sensual, perfect, eternal, and the lower world of our senses, which, though nearer to us, is yet less real than the other, and chiefly important because of the suggestions and hints which it gives of the world of 'Ideas'. Clearly the task of man, with these two worlds before him, is to live as far as possible in the higher, the real, perfect, eternal world, the world of thought, or, as we should say, the spiritual world. *Ex umbris et imaginibus in veritatem.*

5. But this ascent from shadows and images to the truth can only be made by the soul, and the soul is therefore the important thing in man, the part of him which can grasp the world of 'Ideas' and live in it. The body, whose organs are the senses, is always entangled in the lower world of sense, unable to perceive the 'Ideas' and inclined to ignore them. The secret of a successful life is to live as far as possible the life of the soul, communing with the higher, more real, world which it alone can enter.

6. The 'Ideal Theory', then, has two aspects. It is a Theory of Knowledge, an attempt to explain how we know, of which a modern philosopher has said that it is one of the most successful attempts hitherto made.[1] But it is

[1] Bertrand Russell, *The Problems of Philosophy*, p. 142.

also a Theory of Reality, and many people will feel that it gives a fundamentally true account of the world. Here, as in his view of the state in the *Republic*, Plato raises a permanent problem and represents a permanent mode of the human mind. The 'Ideal Theory' is a touchstone to separate out those who do and those who do not believe in the existence of an unseen eternal world from which the visible world draws all its meaning and value.

This was Plato's master work. He created in the intellectual chaos of the fifth century a clear and closely reasoned philosophy of the supremacy of the spiritual life, out of which all later philosophies of the spirit ultimately spring, and which most people will feel to be not only the first but the greatest statement of the belief that the things which are seen are temporal, but the things which are not seen are eternal. Here is the theory of natural religion; here is the threshold of Christianity.

But Plato lived in two worlds; and his intense sense of the world of the spirit drove him on to create a state in which the spiritual life may be possible on earth. Hence his masterpiece, *The Republic* (or *The State*), into which he put all his thought on life and politics and almost all himself—the greatest of all secular prose works, equally remarkable for the wealth and depth of its ideas and for the superb literary art which has combined them into a whole. It is characteristic that its real title is *On Justice*: so far is Plato from the modern view that politics is not concerned with ethics. The aim of the Platonic

State is to embody justice, the condition of its existence that it should succeed in the attempt. It is to be ruled by philosophers (Plato means much more by this word than we do; see p. 89), who, like a religious order, are not permitted to have either private property or family life. Yet, even when he drew this picture of the ideal state, he knew that it was no earthly city. So in later life he wrote his longest work, the *Laws*, in which with much detail and a close eye to actual needs he sketched a second-best but practicable state, 'intended to serve as a guide to the many legislators whom the Academy sent out to revise the constitutions of such Greek states as felt the need of a legislator'.[1] Though an amazing achievement for a man of over 70, the *Laws* has not the literary art of the *Republic*, and details of legislation, designed for a Greek city state, have for the most part only historical interest for us. But it contains much of Plato's ripest wisdom and is especially interesting for its views on education.

Plato's political ideals present one stumbling-block—their authoritarianism. It is only a single element in them and should not distract attention from the rest: and if we are to have an authoritarian state, Plato's is the best form of it. (A glance at the description of the ruling class in the Platonic state (pp. 93 ff.) will show how wholly different it is from modern totalitarianisms.) Still there it is—the belief that a country should be governed and its thought controlled by an *élite*. Authoritarianism is a permanent and

[1] Burnet, *Platonism*, p. 86.

recurring mode of the human mind—at the moment it dominates five European countries. In the motives which led Plato to adopt it—passionate idealism and the remoteness of contemporary Athens from his ideals—we can see the nobler reasons which impel men to such beliefs.

An idealist of genius, after a brief contact with politics, withdraws from them in order by long and close study to determine what the ideal state should be and how it can be created and preserved. There are advantages and risks in such a method. The ship of state so conceived will be nobly designed and amply equipped for its voyage. The city of these dreams will have something of a new Jerusalem, 'descending out of heaven from God and having the glory of God'; and certainly in its ends and aspirations the Platonic republic leaves little to be desired. It is wholly free from the disastrous or ignoble ambitions which have disfigured the states of history, and from the hesitation and vagueness of purpose which have frustrated them. It knows its port of destination and the course to it. So far, so good.

But in a sense the weakness of Plato lies in the nobility of his aim, his absorption in it, his intense desire to create it. He is the type of those reformers and planners who forget that politics deals with men, and that men cannot be manipulated like atoms or cells or even like animals. The material is both too resistant and too fine for such treatment. It rebels and frustrates attempts to coerce it into virtue; and is spoiled even if the attempts are successful. The gravest criticisms against Plato are that he imposes goodness forcibly, that his methods would fail in practice, and that at best they could only produce a mechanical virtue and a static and stereotyped humanity. Plato was a child of the great age of Athenian democracy, which created the ideals of liberty and free speech. Those who believe in them, however greatly they admire his ideals, will not favour some of the means which he employs to achieve them.

Yet his views have never died. He brought into the world one of the great schools of political thought. The authoritarians of all ages are his children—all who from natural pessimism or bitter experience have held that the masses must be saved from themselves by a governing *élite*. At its lowest this ideal appears in modern Russia, Germany, and Italy, whose governing classes have nothing in common with the rulers of the Platonic state, at its highest in the medieval church, whose religious orders, freed from the ties of family life and the temptations of private property and dedicated to the service of a spiritual ideal come, at least in theory, nearest to Plato's 'philosopher kings'.

The variety of his interests, the stimulus of his outlook, the human interest illuminating his abstract thought, his imaginative power, the brilliance of his writing make Plato more suitable for selection than any other philosophical writer. The following passages are a few coins from his wealth. I have not attempted to give a complete view of his philosophy, nor do the extracts under each topic necessarily give a complete account of Plato's views on it. (Thus the passages on sex, p. 184, were chosen to show the error of the common opinion that the Greeks had no idea of spiritual love or sexual purity.) I have avoided the technical and abstruse parts of his philosophy and anything which needs for its understanding special knowledge of Athenian life or Platonic thought. Only one specimen of Socratic cross-examination is given (p. 21 f.), and a good deal of the dialogue which consists in 'Certainly' and 'Yes, Socrates' has been cut: in some cases passages have been shortened.

One difficulty in reading Greek in translation is that there is no English equivalent for certain Greek words. Particularly important are three constantly recurring words, *areté*, *sophrosyné dikaiosyné*.[1] They are generally translated 'virtue', 'temperance', and 'justice', and as there are no English equivalents I have left these renderings, though they are seriously misleading. The reader, when he meets 'virtue', 'temperance' and 'justice' in the text, should realize that they represent far more profound and fruitful conceptions than the English words suggest.

Virtue. To a Greek everything is capable of a 'virtue'. It achieves it, when it is at its best, does the best of which it is capable, serves perfectly the purpose for which it is intended. A knife has a 'virtue'—to cut well. A cow has one—to give good and ample milk. A doctor has one—to cure his patients. A teacher has one—to educate his pupils. A journalist has one

[1] Other misleading words are 'music' (p. 109 n.) and 'spirit' (142 n.).

—to inform and guide the public correctly. An artist has one—to produce good art. So with each thing and creature: each is capable of a 'virtue' of its own. And man is capable of many 'virtues'—as child, parent, citizen, in his profession or occupation, as a human being with a body, character, and intellect (each capable of its peculiar 'virtue' or excellence). The Greek meaning of 'virtue' is well brought out in the *Meno* passage on p. 21.

Temperance is the accepted translation of the word *sophrosyné* which has no English equivalent. *Sophrosyné* is the self-control, balance, sanity, reasonableness, that avoids extremes of action, speech, and thought—a rightness of mind which brings harmony into a personality or a life.[1]

Justice. The meaning of *dikaiosyné* appears from Plato's definition of its opposite. 'I call it injustice, when anger and fear, pleasure and pain, jealousies and desires, tyrannize over the soul.'[2] Clearly 'justice' is a very inadequate description of the Greek word. Perhaps the nearest English equivalent is the old-fashioned word 'righteousness'.

It is hoped that this book will introduce Plato to some persons who do not know him and encourage them to make his closer acquaintance. The obvious dialogues to begin with are the *Apology*, *Crito*, and *Phaedo*. These have been published in an English translation with introduction and notes for the general reader.[3] The

[1] I have attempted a fuller definition of this profound conception in *Portrait of Socrates*, p. liv.

[2] *Laws*, 863.

[3] *Portrait of Socrates*, edited by R. W. Livingstone.

next thing to read is Plato's greatest work, the *Republic*; but it should be read with Nettleship's *Lectures on the Republic*, or some similar book. Without such a guide the reader will misunderstand much of its meaning and miss more.

The standard translation of Plato is Jowett's (Clarendon Press) which is used here (with alterations). There are also good translations of some dialogues in Macmillan's Golden Treasury Series, and of the *Republic* in the Everyman Library. Much the best translation of the *Laws* is by Professor A. E. Taylor. The best introductions to Plato are Professor Taylor's *Plato and His Dialogues*, and *Platonism* (a short book in the 'Our Debt to Greece and Rome' Series); though limited in scope, the brilliant and lucid essay by R. L. Nettleship called *The Theory of Education in Plato's Republic* (Oxford University Press) can also be highly recommended. *Plato* by P. Leon (Discussion Books) is stimulating and suggestive.

CHAPTER I

SOCRATES

Portraits of Socrates

(*a*) *In the army. The speaker is Alcibiades.*

Socrates and I went on the expedition to Potidaea;[1] there we messed together, and I had the opportunity of observing his extraordinary power of sustaining fatigue. His endurance was simply marvellous when we were cut off from our supplies, and compelled to go without food—on such occasions, common enough in time of war, he was superior not only to me but to everybody; there was no one to be compared to him. Yet when we feasted he was the only person who had any real powers of enjoyment; though not willing to drink, he could if compelled beat us all at that,—wonderful to relate! no human being had ever seen Socrates drunk. His fortitude in enduring cold was also surprising. There was a severe frost, for the winter in that region is tremendous, and everybody else either remained indoors, or if they went out had on an immense quantity of clothes, and were well shod, and had their feet swathed in felt and fleeces: in the midst of this, Socrates with his bare feet on the ice and in his ordinary dress marched better than the other soldiers who had shoes, and they looked daggers at him because he seemed to despise them. I have told you one tale, and now I must tell you another of his behaviour

[1] A town near Salonika.

on the expedition. One morning he was thinking about something which he could not resolve; he would not give it up, but continued thinking from early dawn until noon—there he stood fixed in thought; and at noon he was noticed, and the rumour ran through the wondering crowd that Socrates had been standing and thinking about something ever since the break of day. At last, in the evening after supper, some Ionians out of curiosity (I should explain that this was not in winter but in summer), brought out their mats and slept in the open air in order to watch him and see whether he would stand all night. There he stood until the following morning; and with the return of light he offered up a prayer to the sun, and went his way. I will also tell, if you please—and indeed I am bound to tell—of his courage in battle; for who but he saved my life? Now this was the engagement in which I received the prize for courage: for I was wounded and he would not leave me, but he rescued me and my arms; and he ought to have received the prize for courage which the generals wanted to confer on me partly on account of my rank, and I told them so, but he was more eager than the generals that I and not he should have the prize. There was another occasion on which his behaviour was very remarkable—in the flight of the army after the battle of Delium, where he served among the heavy-armed—I had a better opportunity of seeing him than at Potidaea, for I was myself on horseback, and therefore comparatively out of danger. He and Laches were retreating, for the troops were in flight, and I met them and told them not to be discouraged, and promised to remain with them; and there you might see him, just as he is in the streets of Athens, stalking like a pelican, and rolling his eyes, calmly contemplating enemies as well as friends, and making very intelligible to anybody, even from a distance, that whoever attacked him would be likely to meet with a stout resistance; and in this way he and his companion escaped—for this is the sort of man who is never touched in war; those only are pursued who are running away headlong.[1]

(*b*) *At a drinking party. This and the following extracts show characteristic settings of the dialogues.*

Agathon[2] got up to take his place on the seat by Socrates, when suddenly a band of revellers entered, and there was a regular uproar. Some one who was going out having left the door open, they had found their way in, and made themselves at home; great confusion ensued, and every one was compelled to drink large quantities of wine. Aristodemus said that Eryximachus, Phaedrus, and others went away—he himself fell asleep, and as the nights were long took a good rest: he was awakened towards daybreak by a crowing of cocks, and when he awoke, the others were either asleep, or had gone away; there remained only Socrates, Aristophanes, and Agathon, who were drinking out of a large bowl which they passed round, and Socrates was discoursing to them. Aristodemus was only half awake, and he did not hear the

[1] *Symposium*, 219 f.

[2] Agathon was a well-known tragic poet: Aristophanes is the famous comic writer. The Lyceum was a gymnasium.

beginning of the discourse; the chief thing which he remembered was Socrates compelling the other two to acknowledge that the genius of comedy was the same as that of tragedy, and that the true artist in tragedy was an artist in comedy also. To this they were constrained to assent, being drowsy, and not quite following the argument. And first of all Aristophanes dropped off, then, when the day was already dawning, Agathon. Socrates, having laid them to sleep, rose to depart; Aristodemus, as his manner was, following him. At the Lyceum he took a bath, and passed the day as usual. In the evening he retired to rest at his own home.[1]

(*c*) *On a country walk.*

Socrates. My dear Phaedrus, where do you come from, and where are you going?

Phaedrus. I have come from Lysias and I am going for a walk outside the walls, for I have been sitting with him the whole morning; and our common friend Acumenus[2] tells me that it is much more refreshing to walk in the open air than in a cloister.

Soc. There he is right. So Lysias is in town? And what were you talking about? I am sure that he gave you a feast of eloquence.

Phaedr. You shall hear, if you can spare time to accompany me.

Soc. And should I not think the conversation of you and Lysias 'a thing of higher import', as Pindar says, 'than any business'? Let us turn

[1] *Symposium*, 223 f. [2] A famous doctor.

aside and go by the Ilissus; we will sit down at some quiet spot.

Phaedr. I am lucky in not having my sandals, and as you never have any, we may go along the brook and cool our feet in the water; this will be the easiest way, and pleasant too at midday and in the summer.

Soc. Lead on, and look out for a place in which we can sit down.

Phaedr. Do you see that tallest plane-tree in the distance?

Soc. Yes.

Phaedr. There are shade and gentle breezes, and grass on which we can sit or lie.

Soc. Lead on.

Phaedr. Tell me, Socrates, was it not near here that the North Wind is said to have carried off Orithyia from the banks of the Ilissus?

Soc. So they say.

Phaedr. And is this the exact spot? The little stream is delightfully clear and bright—the kind of stream by which girls might play.

Soc. No it was not here, but about a quarter of a mile lower down, where you cross to the temple of Artemis, and there is, I think, some sort of an altar of the North Wind there.

Phaedr. I don't think I know it: but tell me, Socrates, do you believe the story?

Soc. The philosophers doubt it, and I should not be singular if, like them, I too doubted. And then I should have a rational explanation that Orithyia was playing with Pharmacia, when a northern gust carried her over the neighbouring rocks; and so she was killed, and people said that the North Wind had carried her off. Now I quite acknowledge that these rational explanations are charming, but their inventor will need industry and ingenuity, and I do not envy him—if only because next he will have to correct the anatomy of Hippocentaurs, and then of Chimaeras. And then comes a flood of Gorgons and winged horses and unimaginable legendary creatures, equally numerous and bizarre. And if he is sceptical about them, and wants to bring them one after another within the laws of probability, this sort of crude philosophy will take up a great deal of time. Now I have no leisure for such enquiries; shall I tell you why? I must first know myself, as the inscription at Delphi says; it would be absurd to be curious about what is no business of mine, while I don't know my own self. And so I leave all that alone; the common view is enough for me. As I was saying, I study myself instead: am I a monster more complicated and inflamed with passion than the serpent Typho, or a creature of a gentler and simpler sort, to whom Nature has given a more divine and modest destiny? But, if I may interrupt, is not this the plane-tree to which you were guiding us?

Phaedr. Yes, this is the tree.

Soc. What a lovely place to rest, full of summer sounds and scents. Here is this tall, spreading plane-tree, and the agnus castus high and clustering, in the fullness of its blossom and scent; and the stream which flows beneath the plane-tree is ice-cold to the feet. Judging from the ornaments and images, this must be a spot sacred to Achelous and the Nymphs. How delightful is the breeze! how sweet! it makes a shrill and summer music to the chorus of the cicadae. But the great charm is the grass, like a pillow gently sloping to the head. My dear Phaedrus, you have been an admirable guide.

Phaedr. What an incomprehensible being you are, Socrates: when you are in the country, as you say, you are just like a man in the charge of a guide. Do you ever cross the border? I don't believe that you venture even outside the city gates.

Soc. Forgive me, my friend. The reason is that I have a passion for knowledge, and the country and the trees will not teach me anything, but the city people will. Though I do indeed believe that you have found a spell to draw me out of the city into the country, like a hungry cow before whom people wave a bough or a bunch of fruit. So if you will only hold a book before me you may lead me all round Attica, and over the wide world. And now here we are; I shall lie down, and do you choose the position in which you can read best, and begin.[1]

(*d*) *At a festival.*

I went down yesterday to the Piraeus with Glaucon the son of Ariston, to offer up my prayers to the goddess;[2] and also because I wanted to see how they would celebrate the festival, which was a new thing. I was delighted with the local procession; but that of the Thracians was equally, if not more, beautiful. When we had finished our prayers and seen the sight, we turned back to

[1] *Phaedrus*, 227 f.

[2] Bendis, the Thracian Artemis.

Athens: and at that instant Polemarchus the son of Cephalus caught sight of us from a distance as we were starting on our way home, and told his servant to run and tell us to wait for him. The servant took hold of me by the cloak behind, and said: Polemarchus desires you to wait.[1]

They are joined by other friends who had been at the festival, including Glaucon's brother Adeimantus. In Cephalus—a delicate and sympathetic portrait—and those unpleasant Struldbrugs, his elderly friends, we have a glimpse of the ordinary unsophisticated Athenian and of the earthier side of humanism.

Adeimantus said: Has no one told you of the torch-race on horseback in honour of the goddess which will take place in the evening?

With horses! I replied: That is a novelty. Will horsemen carry torches and pass them one to another as they race?

Yes, said Polemarchus, and there will be a festival in the evening which you certainly ought to see. Let us rise soon after supper and see it: there will be a number of young men there, and we will have a good talk.

Accordingly we went with Polemarchus to his house; and there we found Cephalus the father of Polemarchus, whom I had not seen for a long time, and I thought him very much aged. He was seated on a cushioned chair, and had a garland on his head, for he had been sacrificing in the court; and there were some other chairs in the room arranged in a semicircle, upon which we sat down

[1] *Republic*, 327.

by him. He saluted me eagerly, and then he said:—

You don't come to see me, Socrates, as often as you ought: If I were still able to go and see you I would not ask you to come to me. But at my age I can hardly get to the city, and so you should come oftener to the Piraeus. For let me tell you, that the more the pleasures of the body fade away, the greater I find the pleasure and charm of conversation. Do not then deny my request, but make our house your resort and keep company with these young men; we are old friends, and you will be quite at home with us.

I replied: There is nothing that I like better, Cephalus, than talking with the old; I look on them as travellers who have gone a journey, which I too may have to go, and of whom I ought to ask, whether the way is smooth and easy, or rugged and difficult. And this is a question which I should like to ask of you who have arrived at what the poets call the 'threshold of old age'—Is life harder towards the end, or what report do you give of it?

I will tell you, Socrates, he said, what my own feeling is. Men of my age flock together; we are birds of a feather, as the old proverb says; and at our meetings most of us talk regretfully of the pleasures of youth and recall love adventures and drinking parties and feasting and all that sort of thing; there was a good time once, but now that is gone, and life is no longer life. Some complain of the slights which are put upon them by relations, and they will tell you sadly of how many evils their old age is the cause. But to me, Socrates, these complainers seem to blame that which is not really in fault. If old age were the cause, I too, and every other old man, would have felt as they do. But this is not my own experience, nor that of others whom I have known. How well I remember the aged poet Sophocles, when some one asked him, Can you still make love,—are you still capable of sexual pleasure? Peace, he replied; most gladly have I escaped the thing of which you speak; I feel as if I had escaped from a mad and furious master. His words have often occurred to my mind since, and they seem as good to me now as at the time when he uttered them. For certainly old age has a great sense of calm and freedom; when the passions relax their hold, then, as Sophocles says, we are freed from the grasp not of one mad master only, but of many. The truth is, Socrates, that these regrets, and also the complaints about relations, are to be attributed to the same cause, which is not old age, but men's characters and tempers; a calm and happy nature will hardly feel the pressure of age, but to its opposite youth and age are equally a burden.

I listened admiringly, and wanting to draw him out,—Yes, Cephalus, I said; but I rather suspect that people in general are not convinced by you when you speak thus; they think that old age sits lightly upon you, not because of your happy nature, but because you are rich, and wealth is well known to be a great comforter.

You are right, he replied; they are not convinced: and there is something in what they say; not, however, so much as they imagine. I might answer them as Themistocles answered the Seriphian who was abusing him and saying that he was famous, not for his own merits but because he was an Athenian: 'If you had been a native of my country or I of yours, neither of us would have been famous.' And to those who are not rich and are impatient of old age, the same reply may be made; to the good poor man old age cannot be a light burden, nor can a bad rich man ever be at peace with himself.

May I ask, Cephalus, whether your fortune was for the most part inherited or acquired by you?

Acquired! Socrates; do you want to know how much I acquired? In the art of making money I have been midway between my father and grandfather: my grandfather, whose name I bear, doubled and trebled the value of his patrimony, that which he inherited being much what I possess now; but my father reduced the property below its present value: and I shall be satisfied if I leave my sons here not less but a little more than I received.

That was why I asked you the question, I replied, because I see that you are indifferent about money, which is a characteristic rather of those who have inherited their fortunes than of those who have made them; the makers of fortunes have a second love of money as a creation of their own, like the affection of authors for their own poems, or of parents for their children, besides that natural love of it for the sake of use and profit which is common to them and all men. And so they are very bad company, for they can talk about nothing but the praises of wealth. But may I ask another question?—What do you consider to be the greatest blessing which you have reaped from your wealth?

One, he said, of which I could not expect easily to convince others. For let me tell you, Socrates, that when a man thinks himself near death, fears and cares enter into his mind which he never had before; the tales of an after life and the punishment there of deeds done here were once a laughing matter to him, but now he is tormented with the thought that they may be true: either from the weakness of age, or because he is now drawing nearer to that other place, he has a clearer view of these things; suspicions and alarms crowd thickly upon him, and he begins to reflect and consider what wrongs he has done to others. And when he finds that the sum of his transgressions is great he will many a time like a child start up in his sleep for fear, and he is filled with dark forebodings. But if a man is conscious of no sin, sweet hope, as Pindar charmingly says, is the kind nurse of his age:

> 'Hope,' he says, 'cherishes the soul of him who lives in justice and holiness, and is the nurse of his age and the companion of his journey;—hope which is mightiest to sway the restless soul of man.'

What admirable words! And the great blessing of riches, I do not say to every man, but to a good man, is, that he has had no occasion to deceive or to defraud others, either intentionally or unintentionally; and when he passes to the next world he has no anxieties about offerings due to the gods or debts which he owes to men. Now to this peace of mind the possession of wealth greatly contributes; and so I say, that, setting one thing against another, of the many advantages which wealth has to give, to a man of sense this is in my opinion the greatest.

(*e*) *In an Athenian house.*

In this passage we meet leading representatives of the most important and influential intellectual force of the age, the 'Sophists'.

Fifth-century Athens had an advanced democratic régime but no higher education. Hence the appearance of a class of teachers who offered to supply the knowledge and training necessary for the public life in which every Athenian citizen took part. Many of these 'Sophists' or 'wise men', as they were called, were men of genius. Plato disliked them as essentially superficial, and as the cause of still greater superficiality in their hearers. We may understand his attitude if we think of our modern Sophists, men of the type of Shaw, Wells, Aldous Huxley, and Gerald Heard, and of their effect on a partly educated public.

Last night, or rather very early this morning, Hippocrates gave a tremendous thump with his staff at my door; some one opened to him, and he came rushing in and bawled out: Socrates, are you awake or asleep? I knew his voice, and said: Hippocrates, is that you? and do you bring any news? Good news, he said; nothing but good. Delightful, I said; but what is the news? and why have you come here at this unearthly hour? He drew nearer to me and said: Protagoras[1] is come. Yes, I replied; he came two days ago; have you only just heard of his arrival? Yes, by the gods,

[1] A famous sophist.

he said; but not until yesterday evening. At the same time he felt for the truckle-bed, and sat down at my feet, and then he said: Yesterday, when we had done supper and were about to retire to rest, my brother said to me: Protagoras is come. I was going to you at once, and then I thought that the night was far spent. But the moment sleep left me after my fatigue, I got up and came hither direct. I, who knew his fiery excitable temper, said: What is the matter? Has Protagoras robbed you of anything? He replied, laughing: Yes, indeed he has, Socrates, of the wisdom which he keeps from me. But, surely, I said, if you give him money, and make friends with him, he will make you as wise as he is himself. Would to heaven, he replied, that this were the case! He might take all that I have, and all that my friends have, if he pleased. But that is why I have come to you now, in order that you may speak to him for me; for I am young, and also I have never seen nor heard him (when he visited Athens before I was but a child); and all men praise him, Socrates; he is reputed to be the most accomplished of speakers. There is no reason why we should not go to him at once, and then we shall find him at home. He lodges, as I hear, with Callias, the son of Hipponicus: let us start. I replied: Not yet, my good friend; the hour is too early. But let us rise and take a turn in the court and wait about there until day-break; when the day breaks, then we will go.

Later they go to the house where Protagoras is staying, and stop in the porch to finish a discussion.

I think that the door-keeper, who was a eunuch, and who was probably annoyed at the great inroad of Sophists, must have heard us talking. Anyhow, when we knocked at the door, and he opened and saw us, he grumbled: They are Sophists—he is not at home; and at the same time he banged the door to heartily with both his hands. Again we knocked, and he answered without opening: Did you not hear me say that he is not at home, fellows? But, my friend, I said, you need not be alarmed; for we are not Sophists, and we are not come to see Callias, but we want to see Protagoras; and I must request you to announce us. At last, after a good deal of difficulty, the man was persuaded to open the door. When we entered, we found Protagoras taking a walk in the cloister; and next to him, on one side, were walking Callias, the son of Hipponicus, and Paralus, the son of Pericles. On the other side of him were Xanthippus, the other son of Pericles, also Antimoerus of Mende, who of all the disciples of Protagoras is the most famous and intends to make sophistry his profession. A train of listeners followed him; the greater part of them appeared to be foreigners, whom Protagoras had brought with him out of the various cities visited by him in his journeys, he, like Orpheus, attracting them by his voice, and they following. I should mention also that there were some Athenians in the company. Nothing delighted me more than the precision of their movements: they never got into his way at all; but when he and those who were with him turned back, then the band of listeners parted regularly on either side; he was always in front, and they wheeled round and took their places behind him in perfect order. After him, as Homer says, 'I lifted up my eyes and saw' Hippias the Elean sitting in the opposite cloister on a chair of state, and around him were seated on benches strangers whom he had brought with him from his native city of Elis, and some others: they were putting to Hippias certain physical and astronomical questions, and he, *ex cathedra*, was determining their several questions to them, and discoursing of them. Also, 'my eyes beheld Tantalus';[1] for Prodicus the Cean was at Athens: he had been lodged in a room which, in the days of Hipponicus, was a storehouse; but, as the house was full, Callias had cleared this out and made the room into a guest-chamber. Now Prodicus was still in bed, wrapped up in sheepskins and bedclothes of which there seemed to be a great heap. I was very anxious to hear what Prodicus was saying, for he seems to be an all-wise and inspired man; but I was not able to get into the inner circle, and his fine deep voice made an echo in the room which rendered his words inaudible.[2]

The following is a portrait of Hippias, one of the lesser Sophists, mentioned above.

I know, Hippias, that in most arts you are the wisest of men, as I have heard you boasting when you were setting forth the great and enviable stores of your wisdom; and you said that upon one

[1] A quotation from Homer, which continues 'in terrible pain'. The allusion is to the physical condition of P. and perhaps to his love of money—Tantalus being a type of unsatisfied desires. Note the urbane sarcasm with which Plato, no lover of the Sophists, treats them.

[2] *Protagoras*, 310.

occasion, when you went to the Olympic games, all that you had on your person was made by yourself. You began with your ring, which was of your own workmanship, and you said that you could engrave rings; and you had another seal which was also of your own workmanship, and a strigil and an oil flask, which you had made yourself; you said also that you had made the shoes which you had on your feet, and the cloak and the short tunic; but what appeared to us all most extraordinary and a proof of singular skill, was the girdle of your tunic, which, you said, was as fine as the most costly Persian fabric, and of your own weaving; you told us too that you had brought with you poems, epic, tragic, and dithyrambic, as well as prose writings of the most various kinds; and you said that you were a master of true principles of rhythm and harmony and of orthography; and if I remember rightly, there were a great many other accomplishments in which you excelled. I have forgotten to mention the art of mnemonics, which you regard as your special glory, and I dare say that I have forgotten many other things.[1]

Socrates describes his Methods

(*a*) There is a rough and a smooth method in intellectual education. There is the time-honoured mode which our fathers commonly practised towards their sons, and which is still adopted by many—either of roughly reproving their errors, or of gently advising them; these two methods

[1] *Hippias Minor*, 368 f.

may be correctly described as admonition. But some thinkers appear to have arrived at the conclusion that all ignorance is involuntary, and that no one who thinks himself wise is willing to learn anything in the subjects in which he believes himself clever, and that the admonitory sort of instruction gives much trouble and does little good. So they set to work to eradicate the spirit of conceit in another way. They cross-examine a man's words, when he thinks that he is talking sense but really is not, and easily convict him of inconsistencies in his opinions; these they then place side by side, and show that they contradict one another. He, seeing this, is angry with himself, and grows gentle towards others, and thus is entirely delivered from great prejudices and harsh notions, in a way which is most amusing to the hearer, and produces the most lasting good effect on the person who is the subject of the operation. For as the physician considers that the body will receive no benefit from taking food until internal obstacles have been removed, so the purifier of the soul is conscious that his patient will receive no benefit from the application of knowledge until he is refuted, and from refutation learns modesty; he must be purged of his prejudices first and made to think that he knows only what he knows, and no more. For all these reasons, Theaetetus, we must admit that refutation is the greatest and chiefest of purifications, and he who has not been refuted, though he be the King of Persia[1] himself, is in an awful state of impurity; he is uneducated and ugly

[1] The King of Persia, as the greatest potentate known to the Greeks, became a proverbial phrase.

just where purity and beauty are essential to happiness.[1]

(*b*) My art is like that of midwives, but differs from theirs, in that I attend men and not women, and I look after their souls when they are in labour, and not after their bodies: and the triumph of my art is in thoroughly examining whether the thought which the mind of the young man brings forth is a phantom and a lie, or a fruitful and true birth. And like the midwives, I am barren, and the reproach often made against me, that I ask questions of others and have not the wit to answer them myself, is very just—the reason is, that the god compels me to be a midwife, but does not allow me to have children. So I myself am not at all wise, nor have I any invention or child of my own soul to show, but those who talk with me profit. Some of them appear dull enough at first, but afterwards, as our acquaintance ripens, if God is gracious to them, they all make astonishing progress; and this in the opinion of others as well as in their own. It is quite clear that they never learned anything from me; all that they master and discover comes from themselves. But to me and the god they owe their delivery. And the proof of my words is, that many of them in their ignorance, either in their self-conceit despising me, or falling under the influence of others, have gone away too soon; and have not only lost by an ill upbringing the children of whom I had previously delivered them, but have had subsequent miscarriages owing to evil associates, prizing lies and shams more than

[1] *Sophist*, 229 f.

the truth; and they have at last ended by seeing themselves, as others see them, to be great fools. Dire are the pangs which my art is able to arouse and to allay in those who consort with me, just like the pangs of women in childbirth; night and day they are full of perplexity and travail which is even worse than that of the women.[1] So much for them. And there are others, Theaetetus, who come to me apparently having nothing in them; and as I know that they have no need of my art, I coax them into marrying some one, and by the grace of God I can generally tell who is likely to do them good. Many of them I have given away to Prodicus, and many to other inspired sages.[2] I tell you this long story, friend Theaetetus, because I suspect, as indeed you seem to think yourself, that you are in labour—great with some conception. Come then to me, who am a midwife's son and myself a midwife, and do your best to answer the questions which I will ask you. And if I expose your first-born, because I discover upon inspection that the conception which you have formed is a vain shadow, do not quarrel with me on that account, as women do when their first children are taken from them. For I have actually known some who were ready to bite me when I deprived them of a darling folly, they did not see that I acted from goodwill, not knowing that no god is the enemy of man; neither am I their

[1] Socrates does not disguise how painful and even, to a point, sterilizing, is the critical attitude without which truth is not reached.

[2] Socrates abandons to the Sophists people who are fit for nothing better. For Prodicus, see p. 16.

enemy in all this, but it would be wrong for me to admit falsehood, or to stifle the truth.[1]

A specimen of Socratic 'midwifery': a conversation on the meaning of goodness.

Soc. Be generous, Meno, and tell me how you define 'virtue'.

Men. There will be no difficulty, Socrates, in answering your question. Let us take first the 'virtue' of a man—he should know how to administer the state, and in the administration of it to benefit his friends and harm his enemies; and he must also be careful not to suffer harm himself. A woman's 'virtue' may also be easily described: her duty is to look after her house and obey her husband. Every age, every condition of life, young or old, male or female, bond or free, has a different 'virtue': there are 'virtues' numberless, and no lack of definitions of them; for 'virtue' is relative to the actions and ages of each of us in all that we do.

Soc. How fortunate I am, Meno! When I ask you for one 'virtue', you present me with a swarm of them from your store. Suppose that I carry on the figure of the swarm, and ask you, What is the nature of the bee? and you answer that there are many kinds of bees, and I reply: But do bees differ as bees, because there are many and different kinds of them; or are they not rather to be distinguished by some other quality, as for example beauty, size, or shape? How would you answer me?

[1] *Theaetetus*, 150 f.

Men. I should answer that bees do not differ from one another, as bees.

Soc. And if I went on to say: That is what I want to know, Meno; tell me what is the quality in which they do not differ, but are all alike;—would you be able to answer?

Men. I should.

Soc. And so of the 'virtues', however many and different they may be, they have all a common nature which makes them 'virtues'; and on this he who would answer the question, 'What is "virtue"?' would do well to have his eye fixed: Do you understand?

Men. I am beginning to understand; but I do not as yet take hold of the question as I could wish.[1]

After some other definitions which collapse under criticism Meno describes 'virtue' as 'the power of attaining goods'.

Soc. You affirm 'virtue' to be the power of attaining goods? And the goods which you mean are such as health and wealth and the possession of gold and silver, and having office and honour in the state—those are what you would call goods?

Men. Yes, I should include all those.

Soc. Then, according to Meno, 'virtue' is the power of getting silver and gold; and would you add that they must be gained justly, or do you consider this to be of no consequence? And is any mode of acquisition, even if unjust or dishonest, equally to be deemed 'virtue'?

[1] *Meno*, 71 f.

Men. Not 'virtue', Socrates, but vice.

Soc. Then justice or temperance or holiness, or some other part of 'virtue', it would appear, must accompany the acquisition, and without them the mere acquisition of goods will not be 'virtue'.

Men. Why, how can there be 'virtue' without these?

Soc. And the non-acquisition of gold and silver in a dishonest manner for oneself or another, or in other words the want of them, may be equally 'virtue'?

Men. True.

Soc. Then the acquisition of such goods is no more 'virtue' than the non-acquisition and want of them, but whatever is accompanied by justice or honesty is 'virtue', and whatever is devoid of justice is 'vice'.

Men. It cannot be otherwise, in my judgment.

Soc. And were we not saying just now that justice, temperance, and the like, were each of them a part of 'virtue'?

Men. Yes.

Soc. And so, Meno, this is the way in which you mock me.

Men. Why do you say that, Socrates?

Soc. Why, because I asked you to deliver 'virtue' into my hands whole and unbroken, and I gave you a pattern according to which you were to frame your answer; and you have forgotten already, and tell me that 'virtue' is the power of attaining goods justly, or with justice; and justice you acknowledge to be a part of 'virtue'. If so, it follows from your own admissions, that 'virtue' is doing what you do with a part of 'virtue'; for justice and the like are said by you to be parts of 'virtue'.

Men. What of that?

Soc. What of that! Why, did not I ask you to tell me the nature of 'virtue' as a whole? And you are very far from telling me this; but declare every action to be 'virtue' which is done with a part of 'virtue'; as though you had told me and I must already know the whole of 'virtue', and this too when frittered away into little pieces. So, my dear Meno, I fear that I must begin again and repeat the same question: What is 'virtue'? for otherwise, I can only say, that every action done with a part of 'virtue' is 'virtue'; what else is the meaning of saying that every action done with justice is 'virtue'? Ought I not to ask the question over again; for can any one who does not know 'virtue' know a part of 'virtue'?

Men. No; I do not say that he can.

Soc. Then begin again, and answer me, What, according to you, is the definition of 'virtue'?

Men. O Socrates, I used to be told, before I knew you, that you were always yourself doubting and making others doubt; and now you are casting your spells over me, and I am simply getting bewitched and enchanted, and at my wits' end. And if I may jest, you are just like the flat torpedo fish (you look like one too), who paralyses those who come near him and touch him, as you have now paralysed me, I think. For my soul and my tongue are really paralysed, and I do not know how to answer you; and though I have made an infinite variety of speeches about 'virtue' before now, and to many persons—and very good ones they were, as I thought—at this moment I cannot even say what 'virtue' is.[1]

Meno's last words show the effect of a Socratic cross-examination on its victim. The following passages record such examinations and their results.

I went[2] to one who had the reputation of wisdom, and observed him—his name I need not mention; he was a politician whom I selected for examination—and the result was as follows: When I began to talk with him, I could not help thinking that he was not really wise, although he was thought wise by many, and still wiser by himself; and so I tried to explain to him that he thought himself wise, but was not really wise; and the consequence was that he hated me, and so did many others in the audience. So I left him, saying to myself, as I went away: Well, although I do not suppose that either of us has any knowledge of goodness and beauty, I am better off than he is,—for he knows nothing, and thinks that he knows; I neither know nor think that I know. In this latter point I seem to have slightly the advantage of him. Then I went to another who had still higher pretensions to wisdom, and my conclusion was exactly the same. In consequence I made another enemy of him, and of many others besides him. Then I went to one man after another, becoming conscious of the enmity which I provoked, and it distressed and alarmed me: but necessity was laid upon me,—the word of God, I thought, ought to

[1] *Meno*, 78 f.

[2] The Delphic oracle had said that Socrates was the wisest of men. Socrates proceeded to test the truth of this.

be considered first. After the politicians, I went to the poets. And there, I said to myself, you will be instantly detected; now you will find out that you are more ignorant than they are. So I took them some of the most elaborate passages in their own writings, and asked what was the meaning of them—hoping to learn something from them. Will you believe me? I am almost ashamed to confess the truth, but I must say that there is hardly a person present who would not have talked better about their poetry than they did themselves. Then I knew that not by wisdom do poets write poetry,[1] but by a sort of genius and inspiration; they are like diviners or soothsayers who also say many fine things, but do not understand their meaning. The poets appeared to me to be much in the same case; and I further observed that upon the strength of their poetry they believed themselves to be the wisest of men on subjects in which they were not wise. So I went away, conceiving myself to be superior to them for the same reason that I was superior to the politicians. At last I went to the artisans, for I was conscious that I knew nothing at all, and I was sure that they knew many fine things; and here I was not mistaken, for they did know many things of which I was ignorant, and in this they were certainly wiser than I was. But I observed that even the good artisans fell into the same error as the poets;—because they were good workmen they thought that they also knew all sorts of high matters, and this defect in them overshadowed their wisdom; and so I asked myself on behalf of the oracle, whether I would like to

[1] See p. 186 f.

be as I was, neither having their knowledge nor their ignorance, or like them in both; and my reply to myself and to the oracle was that I was better off as I was. This enquiry has led to my having many unpleasant and formidable enemies, and has given occasion to many calumnies. And I am called wise, for my hearers always imagine that I myself possess the wisdom which I find wanting in others: but the truth is that God only is wise; and by his answer he intends to show that the wisdom of men is worth little or nothing; he is not speaking of Socrates, he is only using my name by way of illustration, as if he said, He is the wisest, who, like Socrates, knows that his wisdom is in truth worth nothing. And so I go about the world, obedient to the god, and search and make inquiry into the wisdom of any one, whether citizen or stranger, who appears to be wise; and if he is not wise, then I show him that he is not wise; and my occupation quite absorbs me, and I have no time to give either to any public matter of interest or to any concern of my own, but I am in utter poverty through my service of the god.[1]

These last words reveal the seriousness of purpose which lies behind the Socratic examinations. No missionary ever had a more positive and ardent gospel.

The fear of death is indeed the pretence of wisdom, and not real wisdom, for it is a pretence of knowing the unknown; and no one knows whether death, which men in their fear apprehend to be the greatest evil, may not be the greatest

[1] *Apology*, 21 f.

good. Is not this ignorance of a disgraceful sort, the ignorance which is the conceit that a man knows what he does not know? And in this respect only I believe myself to differ from men in general, and may perhaps claim to be wiser than they are:—that whereas I know but little of the next world, I do not suppose that I know: but I do know that injustice and disobedience to something higher, whether God or man, is evil and dishonourable, and I will never fear or avoid a possible good rather than a certain evil. And so if you let me go now, and are not convinced by Anytus,[1] who said that since I had been prosecuted I must be put to death (otherwise it would have been better never to prosecute me at all); and that if I get off now, your sons will all be utterly ruined by my teaching—if you say to me, Socrates, this time we will not mind Anytus, and you shall be let off, but upon one condition, that you are not to enquire and speculate in this way any more, and that if you are caught doing so again you shall die;—if this was the condition on which you let me go, I should reply: Men of Athens, I honour and love you; but I shall obey God rather than you, and while I have life and strength I shall never cease from the practice and teaching of philosophy, exhorting any one whom I meet and saying to him as my habit is: You, my friend,—a citizen of the great and mighty and wise city of Athens,—are you not ashamed of trying to get as much money and honour and reputation as possible, while remaining careless and indifferent to wisdom and truth and the greatest perfection of

[1] The prosecutor.

your soul? And if the person with whom I am arguing, says: Yes, but I do care; then I do not leave him or let him go at once; but I proceed to interrogate and examine and cross-examine him, and if I think that he has no virtue in him, but only says that he has, I reproach him with undervaluing the greater, and overvaluing the less. And I shall repeat the same words to every one whom I meet, young and old, citizen and alien, but especially to my fellow Athenians, because they are more closely related to me. For know that this is the command of God; and I believe that no greater good has ever happened to Athens than my service to the God. For I do nothing but go about persuading you all, old and young alike, not to take thought for your persons or your properties, but first and chiefly to care about perfecting the soul. I tell you that virtue is not given by money, but that from virtue comes money and every other good of man, public as well as private. This is my teaching, and if this is the doctrine which corrupts the youth, I am a mischievous person. But if any one says that this is not my teaching, he is speaking an untruth. So, Athenians, I say to you, either acquit me or not; but whichever you do, understand that I shall never alter my ways, not even if I have to die many times. If you kill such an one as I am, you will injure yourselves more than you will injure me. Nothing will injure me, not Meletus nor yet Anytus—they cannot, for a bad man is not permitted to injure a better than himself. I do not deny that Anytus may, perhaps, kill him, or drive him into exile, or deprive him of civil rights; and he may imagine, and others may imagine, that he is inflicting a great injury upon him: but there I do not agree. For the evil of doing as he is doing—the evil of unjustly taking away the life of another—is greater far. And now, Athenians, I am not going to argue for my own sake, as you may think, but for yours, that you may not sin against the God by condemning me, who am his gift to you. For if you kill me you will not easily find a successor to me; I am a sort of gadfly, given to the state by God; and the state is a great and noble steed who is slow in his motions owing to his very size, and requires to be stirred into life. I am that gadfly which God has attached to the state, and all day long and in all places am always fastening upon you, arousing and persuading and reproaching you. The proof of my mission is this:—if I had been like other men, I should not have neglected all my own concerns or patiently seen the neglect of them during all these years, and have been doing yours, coming to you individually, like a father or an elder brother, and urging you to care for virtue; such conduct, I say, would be unlike human nature. If I had gained anything, or if I had been paid for my preaching, there would have been some sense in my doing so; but now, as you see, not even the impudence of my accusers dares to say that I have ever taken or asked pay from any one; of that they have no witness. And I have a sufficient witness to the truth of what I say—my poverty.[1]

The above passage and that which follows are taken from the speech of Socrates at his trial. At the age of 70

[1] *Apology*, 29 f.

he was prosecuted by Anytus, a leading democratic politician, and two others on the charge of irreligion and of corrupting the young, was found Guilty by a majority of 60—the jury was probably 500—and was sentenced to death. These are his final words in court after sentence had been passed.

There is great reason to hope that death is a good; for either death is a state of nothingness and utter unconsciousness, or, as men say, there is a change and migration of the soul from this world to another. Now if you suppose that there is no consciousness, but a sleep like the sleep of him who is undisturbed even by dreams, death will be an unspeakable gain. For if a man were to select the night in which his sleep was undisturbed even by dreams, and were to compare with this the other days and nights of his life, and then were to tell us how many days and nights he had passed in the course of his life better and more pleasantly than this one, I think that any one, I will not say a private person, but even the king of Persia will not find many such days or nights, when compared with the others. Now if death is like this, I say that to die is gain; for eternity is then only a single night. But if death is the journey to another place, and there, as men say, all the dead abide, what good, my friends and judges, can be greater than this? If indeed, when the pilgrim arrives in the world below, he is delivered from the professors of justice in this world, and finds the true judges who are said to give judgment there, Minos and Rhadamanthus and Aeacus and Triptolemus, and other sons of God who were righteous in their own life, that pilgrimage will be worth making. What would not a man give if he might talk with Orpheus and Musaeus and Hesiod and Homer?[1] Nay, if this be true, let me die again and again. I myself, too, shall have a wonderful interest in there meeting and talking with Palamedes, and Ajax the son of Telamon, and any other ancient hero who was unjustly sentenced to death; and there will be no small pleasure, I think, in comparing my own sufferings with theirs. Above all, I shall then be able to continue my search into true and false knowledge; as in this world, so also in the next; and I shall find out who is wise, and who pretends to be wise, and is not. What would not a man give to be able to examine the leader of the great Trojan expedition; or Odysseus or Sisyphus, or numberless others, men and women too! What infinite delight would there be in talking with them and asking them questions! In another world they do not put a man to death for asking questions: assuredly not. For besides being happier than we are, they will be immortal, if what is said is true. So, my judges, you too should face death confidently, and reflect on this one truth, that no evil can happen to a good man, either in life or after death. He and his are not neglected by the gods; nor is my own approaching end a matter of mere chance. I see clearly that the time had arrived when it was better for me to die and be released from trouble. And so I am not angry with those who condemned or those who accused me; they

[1] The great poets of legend and history. Palamedes and Ajax were victims of injustice; Odysseus and Sisyphus, types of wisdom or cunning.

have done me no harm, although they did not mean to do me any good; and for this I may gently blame them. But I have a favour to ask them. When my sons are grown up, punish them and trouble them, as I have troubled you, if they seem to care about riches, or anything, more than about virtue; or if they pretend to be something when they are really nothing,—then reprove them, as I have reproved you, for not caring about that for which they ought to care, and thinking that they are something when they are really nothing. And if you do this, both I and my sons will have received justice at your hands. The hour of departure has arrived, and we go our ways—I to die, and you to live Which is better only God knows.[1]

The last scene. Two of the followers of Socrates are talking.

On previous days we had been in the habit of assembling early in the morning at the court in which the trial took place, and which is not far from the prison. There we used to wait talking with one another until the opening of the doors (for they were not opened very early); then we went in and generally passed the day with Socrates. On the last morning we assembled sooner than usual, having heard on the day before when we quitted the prison in the evening that the sacred ship had come from Delos;[2] and so we

[1] *Apology*, 40 f.

[2] The execution could not take place before the return of the mission to the religious festival at the island of Delos.

arranged to meet very early at the accustomed place. On our arrival the jailer who answered the door, instead of admitting us, came out and told us to stay until he called us. 'The Eleven,'[1] he said, 'are now with Socrates; they are taking off his chains, and giving orders that he is to die to-day.' He soon returned and said that we might come in. On entering we found Socrates just released from chains, and Xanthippe,[2] whom you know, sitting by him, and holding his child in her arms. When she saw us she uttered a cry and said, like a woman: 'O Socrates, this is the last time that either you will converse with your friends, or they with you.' Socrates turned to Crito and said: 'Crito, let some one take her home.' Some of Crito's people accordingly led her away, crying out and beating herself. And when she was gone, Socrates, sitting up on the couch, bent and rubbed his leg, saying, as he was rubbing: How singular is the thing called pleasure, and how curiously related to pain, which might be thought to be the opposite of it; for a man never feels both at the same instant, and yet he who pursues either is generally compelled to take the other; their bodies are two, but they are joined by a single head. And I cannot help thinking that if Aesop had remembered them, he would have made a fable about God trying to reconcile their strife, and how, when he could not, he fastened their heads together; and this is the reason why when one comes the other follows: as I know by my own experience now, when after the pain in my leg

[1] Prison officials.
[2] The wife of Socrates.

which was caused by the chain pleasure appears to follow.[1]

Then follows the discussion of the spiritual life and immortality which is the subject of the 'Phaedo', of which these are the concluding words.

So, I say, let a man be confident about his soul, if he has cast away the pleasures and ornaments of the body as alien things which do him harm rather than good, and has pursued the pleasures of knowledge; and has arrayed the soul, not in some foreign dress, but in her own proper jewels, temperance, and justice, and courage, and truth —in these adorned she is ready to go on her journey to another world, when her hour comes. You, Simmias and Cebes, and all other men, will depart some time or other. Me already, as a tragic poet would say, the voice of fate calls. Soon I must drink the poison; and I think that I had better repair to the bath first, in order that the women may not have the trouble of washing my body after I am dead.

When he had done speaking, Crito said: And have you any commands for us, Socrates—anything to say about your children, or any other matter in which we can serve you?

Nothing particular, Crito, he replied: only, as I have always told you, take care of yourselves; that is a service which you may be always doing to me and mine and to all of us, whether you promise to do so or not. But if you have no thought for yourselves, and care not to follow closely what we have said to-day and times past, then, however

[1] *Phaedo*, 59 f.

much you may profess or promise at the moment, it will be of no use.

We will do our best, said Crito: And in what way shall we bury you?

In any way you like; but you must get hold of me, and take care that I do not run away from you. Then he turned to us, and added with a smile:—I cannot make Crito believe that I am the same Socrates who have been talking and arguing; he fancies that I am the other Socrates whom he will soon see, a dead body—and he asks, How shall he bury me? And though I have spoken many words in the endeavour to show that when I have drunk the poison I shall leave you and go to the joys of the blessed,—these words of mine, with which I was comforting you and myself, have had, I see, no effect upon Crito. And I want you to go bail for me to him now, as at the trial he went bail to the judges for me: but let the promise be of another sort; for he was surety for me to the judges that I would stay here, and you must be my surety to him that I shall not stay, but go away and depart; and then he will suffer less at my death, and not be grieved when he sees my body being burned or buried. I would not have him sorrow at my hard lot, or say at the burial, Thus we lay out Socrates, or, Thus we follow him to the grave or bury him; for false words are not only evil in themselves, but they infect the soul with evil. Be of good cheer then, my dear Crito, and say that you are burying my body only, and do with that whatever is usual, and what you think best.

After saying this, he rose and went into a room to bathe; Crito followed him and told us to wait.

So we remained behind, talking and thinking of the subject of our conversation, and also of the greatness of our sorrow; he was like a father whom we were losing, and we were going to be orphans the rest of our lives. When he had taken the bath his children were brought to him—(he had two young sons and an elder one); and the women of his family also came, and he talked to them and gave them a few directions in the presence of Crito; then he dismissed them and returned to us.

Now the hour of sunset was near, for a good deal of time had passed while he was within. When he came out, he sat down with us again after his bath, but not much was said. Soon the jailer, who was the servant of the Eleven, entered and stood by him, saying:—To you, Socrates, whom I know to be the noblest and gentlest and best of all who ever came to this place, I will not impute the angry feelings of other men, who rage and swear at me, when, in obedience to the authorities, I bid them drink the poison—indeed, I am sure that you will not be angry with me; for others, as you are aware, and not I, are to blame. And so good-bye, and try to bear lightly what must needs be—you know my errand. Then bursting into tears he turned away and went out.

Socrates looked at him and said: I return your good wishes, and will do as you bid. Then turning to us, he said, How courteous he is: since I have been in prison he has always been coming to see me, and at times he would talk to me, and was as good to me as he could be, and now see how generously he sorrows on my account. We must do as he says, Crito; so let the cup be brought, if the poison is prepared: if not, let the attendant prepare some.

Yet, said Crito, the sun is still upon the hill-tops, and I know that many take the draught late, and after they receive the warning, dine and drink and sometimes enjoy some love they desire: do not hurry—there is time enough.

Socrates said: Yes, Crito, and they of whom you speak are right in so acting, for they think that they will be gainers by the delay; but I am right in not following their example, for I do not think that I should gain anything by drinking the poison a little later; I should only be ridiculous in my own eyes for sparing and saving a life which is already forfeit. Please then to do as I say, and not to refuse me.

Crito made a sign to the servant, who was standing by; and he went out, and after some time returned with the jailer carrying the cup of poison. Socrates said: My good friend, you are an expert in these matters; what must I do? The man answered: You have only to walk about until your legs are heavy, and then to lie down, and the poison will act. At the same time he handed the cup to Socrates, who very cheerfully and without the least tremor or change of colour or feature, glancing upwards and looking the man full in the face, Echecrates, as his manner was, took the cup and said: What about making a libation[1] out of this cup? May I, or not? The man answered: We only prepare, Socrates, just so much as we think enough. I understand, he said: but I may and must ask the gods to prosper my journey from

[1] The common ritual before drinking.

this to the other world—even so—and so be it according to my prayer. Then raising the cup to his lips, quite readily and cheerfully he drank off the poison. Till then most of us had been able to control our sorrow; but now when we saw him drinking, and saw too that he had finished the draught, we could do it no longer, and in spite of myself my own tears were flowing fast; so that I covered my face and wept, not for him, but at the thought of my own calamity in having to part from such a friend. Nor was I the first; for Crito when he found himself unable to restrain his tears, had got up, and I followed; and at that moment, Apollodorus, who had been in tears all the time, broke out in a loud and passionate cry which made cowards of us all. Socrates alone retained his calmness: What are you doing, you strange people? he said. I sent away the women mainly in order that they might not strike this false note, for I have been told that a man should die in peace. Be quiet then, and have patience. When we heard his words we were ashamed, and checked our tears; and he walked about until, as he said, his legs began to fail, and then he lay on his back, according to the directions, and the man who gave him the poison now and then looked at his feet and legs; and after a while he pressed his foot hard, and asked him if he could feel; and he said, No; and then his leg, and so upwards and upwards, and showed us that he was cold and stiff. Then he felt them again, and said: When the poison reaches the heart, that will be the end. He was beginning to grow cold about the groin, when he uncovered his face, for he had covered himself up, and said: Crito, I owe a cock to Asclepius; will you remember to pay the debt?[1] The debt shall be paid, said Crito; is there anything else? There was no answer to this question; but in a minute or two a movement was heard, and the attendants uncovered him; his eyes were set, and Crito closed his eyes and mouth.

Such was the end, Echecrates, of our friend; of whom I may truly say, that of all the men of his time whom I have known, he was the wisest and justest and best.[2]

[1] Asclepius is the god of health, and the vow is paid on recovery from life's 'fitful fever'.

[2] *Phaedo*, 114 f.

CHAPTER II

THE SPIRITUAL LIFE: LOVE

Plato is as important in the history of religion as in the history of political thought. In him we meet for the first time in western thought a belief in the supremacy of the soul and the spiritual life. He created the philosophy of natural religion.

Have we not found a path of thought which seems to bring us and our argument to the conclusion, that while we are in the body, and while the soul is infected with the evils of the body, our desire will not be satisfied? and our desire is of the truth. For the body is a source of endless trouble to us by reason of the mere requirement of food; and is liable also to diseases which overtake and impede us in the search after reality: it fills us full of loves and lusts, and fears, and fancies of all kinds, and endless nonsense, and in fact takes away from us the power of thinking at all. Whence come wars, and fightings, and factions? whence but from the body and the body's desires? Wars are caused by the love of money, and money has to be acquired for the sake and in the service of the body; and as a result of all these hindrances we have no time to give to philosophy; and, last and worst of all, even if we are at leisure and devote ourselves to some speculation, the body is always breaking in upon us, causing turmoil and confusion in our enquiries, and so upsetting us that we are prevented from seeing the truth.

Experience has shown us that if we would have pure knowledge of anything we must be quit of the body—the soul in herself must behold things in themselves: and then we shall attain the wisdom which we desire, and of which we say that we are lovers; not while we live, but after death; for if while in company with the body, the soul cannot have pure knowledge, one of two things follows—either knowledge is not to be attained at all, or, if at all, after death. For then, and not till then, the soul will be parted from the body and exist in herself alone. In this present life, I reckon that we make the nearest approach to knowledge when we have the least possible intercourse or communion with the body, and are not contaminated with the bodily nature, but keep ourselves pure until the hour when God himself is pleased to release us. And so having got rid of the foolishness of the body we shall be pure and hold converse with the pure, and know of ourselves the clear light everywhere, which is no other than the light of truth. If this be true, there is great reason to hope that when I have come to the end of my journey, I shall attain that which has been the pursuit of my life. So I go on my way rejoicing, and not I only, but every other man who believes that his mind is prepared and purified. True philosophers, Simmias, are always occupied in the practice of dying, and no one finds death so little formidable as they. Look at the matter thus:—if they have been in every way at issue with the body, and are wanting to be alone with the soul, when this desire of theirs is granted, how inconsistent would they be if they trembled and repined, instead of rejoicing at their departure to that place where they hope to gain that which in life they desired—and this was wisdom—and at the same time to be rid of the company of their enemy. Many a man has been willing to go to the world below animated by the hope of seeing there an earthly love, or wife, or son, and talking with them. And will a true lover of wisdom, convinced that only in the world below he can worthily enjoin her, still repine at death? Will he not depart with joy? Surely he will, my friend, if he is a true philosopher. For he will have a firm conviction that there, and there only, he can find wisdom in her purity. And if this be true, he would be very absurd, as I was saying, if he were afraid of death.[1]

When the soul uses the body as an instrument of perception, that is to say, when it uses the sense of sight or hearing or some other sense, she is dragged by the body into the region of the changeable, and wanders and is confused; the world spins round her, and she is like a drunkard, when she touches change. But when she contemplates in herself and by herself, then she passes into the other world, the region of purity, and eternity, and immortality, and unchangeableness, which are her kindred, and with them she ever lives, when she is by herself and is not let or hindered; then she ceases from her erring ways, and being in communion with the unchanging is unchanging. And this state of the soul is called wisdom.[2]

[1] *Phaedo*, 66 f.
[2] Ibid., 79.

Is it likely that the soul, which is invisible, in passing to the place of the true After-world, which like her is invisible, and pure, and noble, and on her way to the good and wise God, whither, if God will, my soul is also soon to go,—that the soul, I repeat, if this be her nature and origin, will be blown away and destroyed immediately on quitting the body, as popular opinion holds? That can never be. The truth rather is, that the soul which is pure at departing and draws after her no bodily taint, having never voluntarily during life had connexion with the body, which she is ever avoiding, herself gathered into herself;—that soul, I say, herself invisible, departs to the invisible world—to the divine and immortal and rational: and when she reaches it, she is secure of bliss and is released from the error and folly of men, their fears and wild passions and all other human ills, and for ever dwells in company with the gods.

But the soul which has been polluted, and is impure at the time of her departure, and is the companion and servant of the body always, and is in love with and fascinated by the body and by the desires and pleasures of the body, until she is led to believe that the truth only exists in a bodily form, which a man may touch and see and taste and use for sexual pleasures, while she hates and fears and avoids that world, which to our eyes is dark and invisible, but which thought and philosophy can grasp—do you suppose that such a soul will depart pure and unalloyed? She is penetrated by the corporeal, which the continual association and constant care of the body have wrought into her nature. And this corporeal element is heavy and weighty and earthy, and by it the soul is depressed and dragged down again into the visible world, because she is afraid of the invisible and of the world below—prowling about tombs and sepulchres, near which, as they tell us, are seen certain ghostly apparitions of souls which have not departed pure, but have a visible element and so are seen.[1]

Then, my friends, if the soul is really immortal, what care should be taken of her, for the sake not only of the portion of time which is called life, but of eternity! And the danger of neglecting her from this point of view does indeed appear to be terrible. If death had only been the end of all, the wicked would have had a good bargain in dying, for they would have been happily quit not only of their body, but of their own evil together with their souls. But now, as the soul is manifestly immortal, there is no release or salvation from evil except the attainment of the highest virtue and wisdom. For the soul on her journey to the world below takes nothing with her but her training and education.[2]

Theod. If you could only persuade everybody, Socrates, as you do me, of the truth of your words, there would be more peace and fewer evils among men.

Soc. Evils, Theodorus, can never pass away; for there must always remain something which is antagonistic to good. They have no place among the gods in heaven, and so of necessity they hover

[1] *Phaedo*, 80 f. [2] *Phaedo*, 107.

around the mortal nature, and this earthly sphere. So we ought to escape from earth to heaven as quickly as we can; and to escape is to become like God, as far as this is possible; and to become like him, is to become holy, just, and wise. But, my friend, you cannot easily convince mankind that they should pursue virtue or avoid vice, not merely in order to seem good, which is the motive given by the world. But the truth is that God is never in any way unrighteous—he is perfect righteousness; and he of us who is the most righteous is most like him. Here is the true sphere of human cleverness, and of human worthlessness and want of manhood. To know this is true wisdom and virtue, and not to know it is manifest folly and vice. All other kinds of apparent wisdom or cleverness in politics are vulgar, in the crafts[1] mechanical. When men behave wrongly or speak or act impiously, it is much best not to call their unscrupulousness clever; for they glory in their shame, and fancy that they are regarded as types of the successful politician instead of being absurdities and mere cumberers of the earth. Let us tell them that they are all the more truly what they do not think they are because they do not know it; for they do not know the penalty of injustice (yet no knowledge is more necessary)—not flogging and death, as they suppose, which are sometimes the lot of the innocent, but a penalty which cannot be escaped.

Theod. What is that?

Soc. There are two patterns eternally set before them; one divine, which is the highest happiness,

[1] The 'arts' or 'crafts' in Plato cover all forms of handwork or manufacture.

one godless, which is the deepest misery: but they do not see this truth, or observe that in their utter folly and infatuation they are growing like the one and unlike the other, by reason of their evil deeds; and the penalty is, that they lead a life answering to the pattern which they are growing like. And if we tell them, that unless they get rid of their 'cleverness' the world of purity will not receive them after death; and that here on earth, they will live ever a life of likeness to their own evil selves, and with evil friends—when they hear this they in their unscrupulous cleverness will fancy that they are listening to the talk of idiots.

Theod. Very true, Socrates.

Soc. Too true, my friend, as I well know; there is, however, one peculiarity in their case: if they have to reason in private about their dislike of philosophy, and if they have the courage to hear the argument out, and do not run away like cowards, they grow at last strangely discontented with their views; their rhetoric fades away, and they become helpless as children.[1]

To Plato the supreme reality is spiritual—the 'ideas' or 'forms', as he calls them (see p. xiii f.) of Beauty, Truth, Justice, and the rest. Highest of these 'ideas' is the 'Idea of the Good'. Plato never defines it, but speaks of it much as religious thinkers speak of God, and in the following passage compares it to the sun. As the sun makes growth and vision possible, so through the 'Idea of the Good' all things exist and are intelligible. It gives meaning and order and goodness to the universe, and through it we can understand the world. The task

[1] *Theaetetus*, 176.

of man is to see, behind the shadows of earth, the eternal spiritual realities and to shape his life by their light.

The simile of the cave is the story of a man's conversion to religion or to any other form of truth. It opens with human beings in their normal state, living among shadows and taking them for reality: then come the stages of conversion—the difficulties and bewilderments of the new outlook, the contempt and hostility of old associates, the amazement of the converted man at their blindness.

Behold! human beings living in an underground cave, which has a mouth open towards the light and reaching all along the cave; here they have been from their childhood, and have their legs and necks chained so that they cannot move, and can only see before them, for the chains prevent them from turning their heads. Above and behind them a fire is blazing at a distance, and between the fire and the prisoners there is a raised way; and you will see, if you look, a low wall built along the way, like the screen which marionette players have in front of them, over which they show the puppets. And you see men passing along the wall carrying all sorts of vessels, and statues and figures of animals made of wood and stone and various materials, which are visible over the wall? Some of them are talking, others silent.

It is a strange scene that you describe, and strange prisoners.

They are like ourselves, I replied; and they see only their own shadows, or the shadows of one another, which the fire throws on the opposite wall of the cave.

True, he said; how could they see anything but

the shadows if they were never allowed to move their heads?

And they only see the shadows of the objects which are being carried past. Suppose further that the prison had an echo which came from the other side, they would imagine when one of the passers-by spoke that the voice which they heard came from the passing shadow. In fact, men in such a position would fancy that the shadows of the objects were the only reality.

And now look again, and see what will naturally follow if the prisoners are released and disabused of their error. At first, when any of them is liberated and compelled suddenly to stand up and turn his neck and walk and look towards the light, he will suffer sharp pains; the glare will distress him, and he will be unable to see the realities of which in his former state he had seen the shadows; and then conceive some one saying to him, that what he saw before was an illusion, but that now, when he is approaching nearer to reality and his eye is turned towards more real existence, he has a clearer vision,—what will be his reply? And you may further imagine that his instructor is pointing to the objects as they pass and requiring him to name them,—will he not be perplexed? Will he not fancy that the shadows which he previously saw are truer than the objects which are now shown to him? And if he is compelled to look straight at the light, will he not have a pain in his eyes which will make him turn away to the shadows which he can see, and which he will conceive to be in reality clearer than the things which are now being shown to him? And suppose once more, that he is reluctantly dragged up a steep and rugged ascent, and not released until he is forced into the presence of the sun itself, is he not likely to be hurt and annoyed? When he approaches the light his eyes will be dazzled, and he will not be able to see anything at all of what are now called realities. He will have to grow accustomed to the sight of the upper world. And first he will see the shadows best, next the reflections of men and other objects in water, and after that the objects themselves; then he will gaze upon the light of the moon and the stars; and he will see the sky and the stars by night better than he sees the sun or the light of the sun by day. Last of all he will be able to see the sun, and not mere reflections of it in the water, but he will see it in its own proper place; and he will contemplate it as it is. He will then proceed to argue that this is the power that gives the seasons and the years, and is the guardian of all that exists in the visible world, and in a sense the cause of all things which he and his fellows have been accustomed to see. And when he remembered his old home, and what passed for wisdom in the cave with his fellow-prisoners, do you not suppose that he would congratulate himself on the change, and pity them? And if they were in the habit of conferring honours and distinctions and rewards among themselves on those who were quickest to observe the passing shadows and to remark which preceded, and which came after, and which were together; and who were therefore best able to draw conclusions as to the future, do you think that he would care for such honours and glories, or envy the possessors of them? Would he not say with Homer,

> Better to be the poor servant of a poor master,

and to endure anything, rather than think as they do and live after their manner?

Imagine once more, I said, such a person descending to the cave and taking his old seat there; would he not be certain, coming suddenly out of the sunlight, to have his eyes dazzled and blind?

And if there were a competition, and he had to compete in measuring the shadows with the prisoners who had never moved out of the den, while his sight was still weak, and before his eyes had become steady, would he not be ridiculous? Men would say of him that up he went and down he came without his eyes; and that it was better not even to think of ascending; and if any one tried to set free another and lead him up to the light, let them only catch the offender, and they would put him to death.

And now to apply my allegory. The prison-house is the world of sight, the light of the fire is the sun, and you will not misapprehend me if you interpret the journey upwards to be the ascent of the soul into the intellectual world according to my poor belief, which, at your desire, I have expressed—whether rightly or wrongly God knows. But, whether true or false, my opinion is that in the world of knowledge the Idea of Good appears last of all, and is seen only with an effort; and, when seen, is also inferred to be the universal author of all things beautiful and right, parent of light and of the lord of light in this visible world, and the immediate source of reason and truth in the intellectual; and that this is the power upon which he who would act rationally either in public or private life must have his eye fixed.[1]

The path to the knowledge of Reality lies through discipline of character and intellectual training (largely in the sciences and in philosophy). But there is also an approach through Beauty in its many forms. Of all the 'ideas' Beauty has the most universal and strongest appeal, and the beauty of earth moves men because it is a reflection of an Eternal Beauty and wakes the sense of it in them. This view appears in the following passage where Plato portrays the history of the human soul under the image of a chariot with two horses—the noble and the ignoble passions—driven by the charioteer Reason. He describes the soul's pre-natal vision of heavenly things; its incarnation in a higher or lower human nature according as it saw more or less of heaven; its partial recollection of the true heavenly beauty when it meets beauty on earth. Hence comes love, which is the growing of the wings of the soul in the presence of beauty, and in which the ideal or sensual elements predominate, according as the lover is ruled by the orderly element of reason or the disorderly element of desire.

The doctrine of pre-existence and reincarnation, that occurs in the following passage, is taken from the current Orphic creed which colours much of Plato's thought. Though he uses its language, there is no reason to think that he accepted its belief literally: rather, like the modernist with Christian dogma, he believed that Orphic doctrines embodied spiritual truth, expressing in concrete form the certainty of the existence of a spiritual world

[1] *Republic*, 514 f.

to which the soul belongs and in which it realizes its true nature.

The nature of the soul is altogether a subject for large and more than mortal discourse, but to say what the soul resembles is a briefer and human theme. Let me compare it to a pair of winged horses and a charioteer. Now the winged horses and the charioteers of the gods are all of them noble and of noble descent, but those of other races are mixed; our human charioteer drives his in a pair; and one of them is noble and of noble breed, and the other is ignoble and of ignoble breed; and the driving of them is necessarily hard and difficult. I will try to explain to you how the mortal differs from the immortal creature. The soul in her totality has the care of all soulless being, and traverses the whole heaven taking different forms;—when perfect and fully winged she soars upward, and orders the whole world; while the imperfect soul, losing her wings and drooping in her flight at last settles on the solid ground—there, finding a home, she receives an earthly body which appears to be self-moved, but is really moved by her power; and this composition of soul and body is called a living and mortal creature. For immortal no such union can be reasonably believed to be; although our fancy, not having seen nor adequately known the nature of God, may imagine an immortal creature having both a body and also a soul which are united throughout all time. Let that, however, be as God wills, and may our account of it be acceptable to him. And now let us ask the reason why the soul loses her wings!

The wing is the corporeal element which is most akin to the divine, and which by nature tends to soar aloft and carry that which gravitates downwards into the upper region, where the gods dwell. The divine is beauty, wisdom, goodness, and the like; and by these the wing of the soul is nourished, and grows apace; but when fed upon evil and ugliness and the opposite of good, it wastes and is destroyed. Zeus, the mighty leader, holding the reins of a winged chariot, leads the way in heaven, ordering all and taking care of all; and there follows the array of gods and demigods, marshalled in eleven bands; Hestia[1] alone abides at home in the house of heaven; of the rest they who are reckoned among the princely Twelve[2] march in their appointed order. They see many blessed sights in the inner heaven, and there are many ways to and fro, along which the blessed gods are passing, every one doing his own work; he may follow who will and can, for jealousy has no place in the celestial choir. But when they go to banquet and festival, then they move up the steep to the top of the vault of heaven. The chariots of the gods in even poise, obeying the rein, glide rapidly; but the others labour, for the vicious steed goes heavily, weighing down the charioteer to the earth when his steed has not been thoroughly trained:—and this is the hour of agony and extremest conflict for the soul. For the immortals, when they reach the summit, go forth and stand upon the outside of heaven, and the revolution of the spheres carries them round, and they behold

[1] Goddess of the hearth.

[2] The twelve greater gods of the Greek Pantheon.

the things beyond. But of the heaven which is above the heavens, what earthly poet ever did or ever will sing worthily? It is such as I will describe; for I must dare to speak the truth, when truth is my theme. There abides the Very Being with which true knowledge is concerned; the colourless, formless, intangible essence, visible only to mind, the pilot of the soul. The divine intelligence, nurtured upon mind and pure knowledge, and the intelligence of every soul which is capable of receiving the food proper to it, rejoices at beholding Reality, and once more gazing upon Truth, is replenished and made glad, until the revolution of the worlds brings her round again to the same place. In the revolution she beholds Justice, and Self-control, and Knowledge Absolute, not in the form of generation or of relation, which men call existence, but Knowledge Absolute in Existence Absolute; and beholding the other true Existences in like manner, and feasting upon them, she passes down into the interior of the heavens and returns home; and there the charioteer putting up his horses at the stall, gives them ambrosia to eat and nectar to drink.

Such is the life of the gods; but of other souls, that which follows God best and is most like him lifts the head of his charioteer into the outer world, and is carried round in the revolution, troubled indeed by the steeds, and with difficulty beholding true Being; while another now rises, now sinks, and sees, and again fails to see, because its horses are unruly. The rest of the souls are also longing after the upper world and they all follow, but not being strong enough they are carried round below the surface, plunging, treading on one another, each striving to be first; and there is confusion and perspiration and the extremity of effort; and many of them are lamed or have their wings broken through the bad driving of the charioteers; and all of them after much toil, fail to attain to the mysteries of true Being, and go away, and feed upon opinion.[1] The reason why the souls exhibit this intense eagerness to behold the plain of truth is that pasturage is found there, which is suited to the highest part of the soul; and the wing on which the soul soars is nourished with this. And there is a law of Destiny, that the soul which attains any vision of truth in company with a god is preserved from harm until the next period, and if attaining always is always unharmed. But when she is unable to follow, and fails to behold the truth, and through some ill-hap sinks beneath the double load of forgetfulness and vice, and her wings fall from her and she drops to the ground, then the law ordains that this soul shall at her first birth pass, not into any other animal, but only into man; and the soul which has seen most of truth shall come to the birth as a philosopher, or artist, or some musical and loving nature; that which has seen truth in the second degree shall be some law-abiding king or soldier or ruler; the soul which is of the third class shall be a politician, or business man, or financier; the fourth shall be a lover of athletics, or a physician; the fifth shall lead the life of a prophet or hierophant; to the sixth the character of a poet or some other imitative artist will be assigned; to the seventh the life of an artisan or

[1] As opposed to knowledge.

husbandman; to the eighth that of a sophist or demagogue; to the ninth that of a despot;—all these are states of probation, in which he who lives justly improves, and he who lives unjustly, deteriorates his lot.

Ten thousand years must elapse before the soul of each one can return to the place from which she came, for she cannot grow her wings in less; only the soul of a philosopher, guileless and true, or the soul of a lover, who is not devoid of philosophy, may acquire wings in the third of the recurring periods of a thousand years; and they who choose this life three times in succession have wings given them, and go away at the end of three thousand years. But the others[1] are judged when they have completed their first life, and after judgment they go, some of them to the houses of correction which are under the earth, and are punished; others are lightly borne by justice to some place in heaven, and there they live in a manner worthy of the life which they led here when in the form of men. And at the end of the first thousand years the good souls and also the evil souls both come to draw lots and choose their second life, and they may take any which they please. The soul of a man may pass into the life of a beast, or from the beast return again into the man. But the soul which has never seen the truth will not pass into the human form. For a man must have intelligence of universals, and be able to proceed from the many particulars of sense to one conception of reason;—this is the recollection of those things

[1] The philosopher alone is not subject to judgment, for he has never lost the vision of truth.

which our souls once saw while following God—when regardless of that which we now call reality she raised her head up towards Reality itself. And so the mind of the philosopher alone has wings; and this is just, for he is always, according to the measure of his abilities, clinging in recollection to those things in which God abides, and in beholding which He is what He is. And he who rightly uses these memories is ever being initiated into perfect mysteries and alone becomes truly perfect. But, as he forgets earthly interests and is rapt in the divine, most men think him mad, and condemn him; they do not see that he is inspired.

Thus far I have been speaking of the fourth and last kind of madness. In this, when a man sees the beauty of earth, he remembers the true beauty. Wings come to him and, with them, the desire to soar, but not the power; like a bird he gazes towards heaven and forgets earth, and is thought to be mad. And I have shown this of all inspirations to be the noblest and highest and the offspring of the highest to him who has or shares in it, and that he who loves the beautiful is called a lover because he shares it. For, as has been already said, every soul of man has in the way of nature looked on True Being; this was the condition of her passing into the form of man. But all souls do not easily recall the things of the other world; they may have seen them for a short time only, or they may have been unfortunate in their earthly lot, and, having had their hearts turned to unrighteousness through some corrupting influence, they may have lost the memory of the holy things which once they saw. Few only retain an adequate remembrance of them; and they, when they see here any image of that other world, are rapt in amazement; but they are ignorant of what this rapture means, because they do not clearly perceive. For there is no light of Justice or Temperance or any of the other jewels of the soul in their earthly copies: they are seen through a glass dimly; and there are few who, going to the images, behold in them the realities, and these only with difficulty. Yet once the beauty was clear to see, when in that happy company—you and I following in the train of Zeus, others in company with other gods—our souls saw the beatific vision and were initiated into what may be called the most blessed of mysteries, celebrated by us in our state of innocence, while we were untouched by evils to come, when we were admitted to the sight of visions innocent and simple and calm and happy, which we beheld shining in pure light; and we were pure ourselves and unstained by that which we carry about and call our body, imprisoned like shell-fish in their shell. Let me linger over the memory of scenes which passed away.

But of beauty, I repeat again that we saw her there shining in company with the celestial forms; and coming to earth we find her here too, shining in clearness through the clearest aperture of sense. For sight is the most piercing of our bodily senses; though not by that is Wisdom seen; her loveliness would have been transporting if there had been a visible image of her, and the other Ideas, if they had visible counterparts, would be equally lovely. But this is the privilege of beauty, that being the loveliest she is also the most palpable to sight.

Now he who is not newly initiated or who has become corrupted, does not easily rise out of this world to the sight of true Beauty in the other; he looks only at her earthly namesake, and instead of being awed at the sight of her, he is given over to pleasure, and like a brutish beast he rushes on to enjoy and beget. But he whose initiation is recent, and who has been the spectator of many glories in the other world, is amazed when he sees any one having a godlike face or form, which is the expression of divine beauty; and at first a shudder runs through him, and again the old awe steals over him; then looking upon the face of his beloved as of a god he reverences him, and if he were not afraid of being thought a downright madman, he would sacrifice to his beloved as to the image of a god; then while he gazes on him there is a sort of reaction, and the shudder passes into an unusual heat and perspiration; for, as he receives the effluence of beauty through the eyes, blood courses through the wing and he warms.[1]

The Symposium *develops further the idea that beauty and the love which it arouses is a pathway to reality, or, as Plato puts it, a 'mediator between god and man'. Love in the passage that follows is the active principle of the human spirit, a mixed being 'half dust, half deity', drawing purely human elements from his mother, Poverty, but from his father, Enterprise (the son of Intelligence), a higher nature which 'desires the everlasting possession of good'. Man 'falls in love' with human beauty and from that rises to other loves—love of the beauty of character and action and law and great*

[1] *Phaedrus*, 246 f.

institutions, and finally of Beauty itself. With this passion is coupled a creative instinct, that is aroused by contact with beauty and then issues in creation on different planes—bringing forth at the physical level children of the body and at higher levels children of the soul.

Plato puts his words on the lips of a Mantinean prophetess, Diotima, with whom Socrates as a young man is supposed to have talked.

'What then is Love?' I asked; 'Is he mortal?' 'No.' 'What then?' 'He is neither mortal nor immortal, but something between the two.' 'What is he, Diotima?' 'He is a great spirit, and like all spirits he is intermediate between the divine and the mortal.' 'And what,' I said, 'is his power?' 'He interprets,' she replied, 'between gods and men, conveying and taking across to the gods the prayers and sacrifices of men, and to men the commands and replies of the gods; he is the mediator who spans the chasm which divides them, and therefore in him all is bound together, and through him the arts of the prophet and the priest, their sacrifices and mysteries and charms, and all prophecy and incantation, find their way. For God mixes not with man; but through Love all the intercourse and converse of God with man, whether awake or asleep, is carried on. The wisdom which understands this is spiritual; all other skills, such as that of arts and handicrafts, are mean and vulgar. Now these spirits or intermediate powers are many and various, and one of them is Love.' 'And who,' I said, 'was his father, and who his mother?' 'It is a rather long story,' she said, 'but I will tell you.

On the birthday of Aphrodite there was a feast of the gods, at which the god Poros or Enterprise, who is the son of Metis or Intelligence, was one of the guests. When the feast was over, Penia or Poverty came to the door to beg. Now Plenty, who was the worse for nectar (there was no wine in those days), went into the garden of Zeus and fell into a heavy sleep; and Poverty considering her own straitened circumstances, plotted to have a child by him, and accordingly she lay down at his side and conceived Love, who partly because he is naturally a lover of the beautiful, and because Aphrodite is herself beautiful, and also because he was born on her birthday, is her follower and attendant. And as his parentage is, so also are his fortunes. In the first place he is always poor, and anything but tender and fair, as popular opinion fancies; and he is rough and unkempt, and has no shoes, and no house to live in; on the bare earth exposed he lies under the open heaven, and sleeps in the streets, or at the doors of houses; and like his mother he is always in distress. Like his father too, whom he also partly resembles, he is always plotting against the fair and good; he is bold, enterprising, strong, a mighty hunter, always weaving some intrigue or other, keen in the pursuit of wisdom, fertile in resources; a philosopher at all times, terrible as an enchanter, sorcerer, sophist. He is by nature neither mortal nor immortal, but alive and flourishing at one moment when he is in plenty, and dead at another moment, and again alive by reason of his father's nature. He is always getting, and always losing what he gets, so he is never either rich or poor: and, further, he is in an intermediate state between ignorance and knowledge. The truth of the matter is this: No god is a philosopher or seeker after wisdom, for he is wise already; and no man who is wise seeks after wisdom. Neither do the ignorant seek after it. For the curse of ignorance is, that a man without being either good or wise is nevertheless satisfied with himself: he has no desire for that of which he feels no want.' 'But who then, Diotima,' I said, 'are the lovers of wisdom, if they are neither the wise nor the foolish?' 'A child may answer that question,' she replied; 'they are those who are between the two; Love is one of them. For wisdom is a most beautiful thing, and Love is of the beautiful; and so Love is also a philosopher or lover of wisdom, and, because he loves it, is in a state between wisdom and ignorance. And this is partly due to his origin, for his father is wealthy and wise, and his mother poor and foolish. Such, my dear Socrates, is the nature of the spirit Love.' 'Well said,' I answered; 'but, assuming Love to be such as you say, what is the use of him to men?' 'That, Socrates,' she replied, 'I will attempt to unfold: of his nature and birth I have already spoken; and you acknowledge that love is of the beautiful. But some one will say: Of the beautiful in what, Socrates and Diotima?—or rather let me put the question more clearly, and ask: When a man loves the beautiful, what does he desire?' I answered her 'To possess it.' 'Still,' she said, 'the answer suggests a further question: What is given by the possession of beauty?' 'To what you have asked,' I replied, 'I have no answer ready.' 'Then,' she said, 'let me put the word "good" in the place of "beautiful", and repeat the question once more: If he who loves loves the good, what is it then that he loves?' 'The possession of the good,' I said. 'And what does a man gain who possesses the good?' 'Happiness,' I replied; 'there is less difficulty in answering that question.' 'Yes,' she said, 'the essence of happiness is the possession of what is good, and there is no need to ask why a man desires happiness; the answer is already final.' 'You are right,' I said. 'And is this wish and this desire common to all? and do all men always desire their own good, or only some men?—what say you?' 'All men,' I replied; 'the desire is universal.' 'Then,' she said, 'the simple truth is, that men love the good and love to possess it and to possess it always. So love may be described generally as the love of the everlasting possession of the good?' 'That is most true.'

'Then if this is love, can you tell me further,' she said, 'what is this quest? what is the goal of all this intense eagerness and heat which is called love? and what is the object which they have in view? Answer me.' 'If I had known, Diotima,' I replied, 'I should not have admired your wisdom, or come to study this very question at your feet.' 'Well,' she said, 'I will teach you:—The object which they have in view is birth in beauty, whether of body or soul.' 'I do not understand you,' I said; 'the oracle needs explanation.' 'I will make my meaning clearer,' she replied. 'I mean to say, that all men are pregnant in their bodies and in their souls. There is a certain age at which human nature is desirous of procreation—procreation which must be in beauty and not in deformity—for conception and generation are an immortal principle of the mortal creature, and in the inharmonious they can never be. But the deformed is always inharmonious with the divine, and the beautiful harmonious. Beauty, then, is the destiny or goddess of parturition who presides at birth, and so, when approaching beauty, the conceiving power is propitious, and diffusive, and benign, and begets and bears fruit: at the sight of ugliness she frowns and contracts and has a sense of pain, and turns away, and shrivels up, and not without a pang refrains from conception. And this is the reason why, when the hour of conception arrives, and the teeming nature is full, there is such a flutter and ecstasy about beauty whose approach is the alleviation of the pain of travail. For love, Socrates, is not, as you imagine, the love of the beautiful only.' 'What then?' 'It is the love of generation and of birth in beauty.' 'Yes,' I said. 'Yes, indeed,' she replied. 'But why of generation?' 'Because to the mortal creature, generation is a sort of eternity and immortality,' she replied; 'and if, as has been already admitted, love is of the everlasting possession of the good, all men will necessarily desire immortality together with good: So love is love of immortality.'

All this she taught me at various times when she spoke of love. And I remember her once saying to me, 'What is the cause, Socrates, of love, and the desire that goes with it? Do you not see how all animals, birds as well as beasts, in their desire of procreation, are in agony when they take the infection of love. It begins with the sexual desire;

and then comes the care of offspring, for which the weakest creatures are ready to fight against the strongest, and to die for them, and will let themselves be tormented with hunger or suffer anything in order to maintain their young. Man may be supposed to act thus from reason; but why should animals have these passionate feelings? Can you tell me why?' 'I have told you already, Diotima, that I come to you because I want to be taught; tell me then the cause of this and of the other mysteries of love.' 'Do not be surprised,' she said, 'if you believe that love is of the immortal, as we have several times agreed; for here again, and on the same principle too, the mortal nature is seeking as far as is possible to be everlasting and immortal: and this is only to be attained by generation, because generation always leaves behind a new existence in the place of the old. Even in the life of the same individual there is succession and not absolute unity: a man is said to preserve his identity, and yet in the short interval which elapses between youth and age he is undergoing a perpetual process of loss and reparation—hair, flesh, bones, blood, and the whole body are always changing. This is true not only of the body, but also of the soul, whose habits, tempers, opinions, desires, pleasures, pains, fears, never remain the same in any one of us, but are always coming and going; it is equally true of knowledge, and what is still more surprising to us mortals, not only do the sciences in general spring up and decay, so that our attitude to them changes; but each of them individually experiences a like change. In this way, Socrates, the mortal body, or any mortal thing, partakes of immortality; there is no other way in which it can do it. Be not surprised then at the love which all men have of their offspring; for that universal love and interest is for the sake of immortality.'

I was astonished at her words, and said: 'Is this really true, wise Diotima?' And she answered with all the authority of an accomplished teacher: 'Of that, Socrates, you may be assured;—think only of the ambition of men, and you will wonder at the senselessness of their ways, unless you consider how they are stirred by the love of an immortality of fame. They are ready to run all risks greater far than they would have run for their children, and to spend money and undergo any sort of toil, and even to die, for the sake of leaving behind them a name which shall be eternal. I am convinced the aim of all men's actions—and the better they are, the more this is true—is the glorious fame of immortal virtue; they desire immortality.'

'Those who are pregnant in the body only, turn to women and beget children—this is their type of love; their offspring, as they hope, will preserve their memory and give them the blessedness and immortality which they desire in the future. But souls which are pregnant—for there certainly are men whose souls are more creative than their bodies—conceive that which is proper for the soul to conceive or contain. And what are these conceptions?—wisdom and virtue in general. And such creators are poets and all artists who deserve to be called original. But far the greatest and most beautiful kind of creation is concerned with the ordering of states and families; and this is called temperance and justice. And a young man who has the seed of these sown in him and is himself inspired, when he comes to maturity longs to beget and generate.[1] He wanders about looking for beauty in order to beget offspring—for in deformity he will beget nothing—and naturally embraces the beautiful rather than the ugly body; above all when he finds a fair and noble and gifted soul, he embraces ardently this union of graces and he talks eagerly to their possessor about the character and life of the good man, and tries to educate him. Present and absent he remembers him and at the touch and company of his beauty brings to birth what he had long ago conceived, and with his friend brings up that child, so that the intimacy of the two is far closer and their friendship firmer than with those who beget mortal children, for the children who are their common offspring are fairer and more immortal. Who, when he thinks of Homer and Hesiod and other great poets, would not rather have their children than ordinary human ones? Who would not emulate them in the creation of children such as theirs, which have preserved their memory and given them everlasting glory? Or who would not have such children as Lycurgus left behind him to be the saviours not only of Lacedaemon, but one might say of Greece? There is Solon, too, who is the honoured father of Athenian laws; and many others there are in many other places, both among Greeks and foreign peoples, who have given to the world many noble works, and have been the parents of virtue of

[1] What follows is a picture of a Greek friendship.

every kind; and many temples have been raised in their honour for the sake of children such as theirs; which were never raised in honour of any one, for the sake of mortal children.

'These are the lesser mysteries of love, into which even you, Socrates, may enter; I do not know if you will be able to attain the greater and more advanced ones which are the final cause of these, if they are rightly pursued. But I will do my utmost to inform you, and do you follow if you can. He who wishes to approach love rightly should turn in youth to beautiful forms, and first love one such form only—out of that he should create fair thoughts; and soon he will of himself perceive that the beauty of one form is akin to the beauty of another; and then if beauty of form in general is his pursuit, how foolish would he be not to recognize that the beauty in every form is one and the same! And when he perceives this he will cease to concentrate his love on a single object—that will seem foolish and petty to him—and will become a lover of all beautiful forms; in the next stage he will consider that the beauty of the mind is more honourable than the beauty of the outward form. So that if he meets someone with few charms of person but whose nature is beautiful, he will be content to love and care for him, and will bring to birth thoughts which make youth better, until he is compelled to contemplate and see the beauty of institutions and laws, and to understand that the beauty of them all is akin, and that personal beauty is a trifle; and after laws and institutions he will go on to the sciences, that he may see their beauty, and not be like a servant in love with the beauty of one youth or man or institution, slavish, mean, and petty, but drawing towards and contemplating the vast sea of beauty, he will create many fair and lofty thoughts and notions in boundless love of wisdom; until on that shore he grows great and strong, and at last the vision is revealed to him of a single science, which is the science of beauty everywhere. And now try, she said, to give me all your mind.

'He who has been instructed so far in the mystery of love, and who has learned to see the beautiful correctly and in due order, when he comes toward the end will suddenly perceive a wondrous beauty (and this, Socrates, is the final cause of all our former toils). It is eternal, uncreated, indestructible, subject neither to increase or decay; not like other things partly beautiful, partly ugly; not beautiful at one time or in one relation or in one place, and deformed in other times, other relations, other places; not beautiful in the opinion of some and ugly in the opinion of others. It is not to be imagined as a beautiful face or form or any part of the body, or in the likeness of speech or knowledge: it does not have its being in any living thing or in the sky or the earth or any other place. It is Beauty absolute, separate, simple, and everlasting, which without diminution, and without increase, or any change, is imparted to the ever-growing and perishing beauties of all other things. If a man ascends from these under the influence of the right love of a friend, and begins to perceive that beauty, he may reach his goal. And the true order of approaching the mystery of love is to begin from the beauties of earth and mount upwards for the sake of that other beauty, using these as steps only, and from one going on to two, and from two to all beautiful forms, and from beautiful forms to beauty of conduct, and from beauty of conduct to beauty of knowledge, until from this we arrive at the knowledge of absolute beauty, and at last know what the essence of beauty is. This, my dear Socrates,' said the stranger of Mantineia, 'is the life above all others which man should live, in the contemplation of beauty absolute; a beauty which if you once beheld, you would see not to be after the measure of gold, and dress, and fair boys and youths, whose sight now entrances you (and you and many others would be content to live seeing them only and talking with them without food or drink, if that were possible—you only want to look at them and to be with them). But what if man had eyes to see the true beauty—the divine beauty, I mean, pure and clear and unalloyed, not clogged with the pollutions of mortality and all the colours and vanities of human life—gazing on it, in communion with the true beauty simple and divine? Remember how in that communion only, beholding beauty with the eye of the mind, he will be able to bring forth, not shadows of beauty, but its truth, because it is no shadow that he grasps, but the truth; and he will give birth to true virtue and nourish it and become the friend of God and be immortal as far as mortal man may. Would that be an ignoble life?'

Such, Phaedrus, were the words of Diotima; and I am convinced of their truth. And being convinced of them, I try to convince others, that in the attainment of this end human nature will not easily find a helper better than love.[1]

Another view of love. The speaker is the great comic poet, Aristophanes.

The sexes were not two as they are now, but originally three in number; there was man, woman, and a combination of the two. The primeval man was round, his back and sides forming a circle; and he had four hands and four feet, one head with two faces, looking opposite ways, set on a round neck and precisely alike; also four ears, two privy members, and the remainder to correspond. He could walk upright as men now do, backwards or forwards as he pleased, and he could also roll over and over at a great pace, turning on his four hands and four feet, eight in all, like tumblers going over and over with their legs in the air; this was when he wanted to run fast. Now the sexes were three, and such as I have described them; because the sun, moon, and earth are three; and the man was originally the child of the sun, the woman of the earth, and the man-woman of the moon, which is made up of sun and earth, and they were all round and moved round and round like their parents. Terrible was their might and strength, and they had proud thoughts, and they made an attack upon the gods; of them is told the tale of Otys and Ephialtes who, as Homer says, dared to scale heaven, and would have laid hands upon the gods. Doubt reigned in the celestial councils. Should they kill them and annihilate the race with thunderbolts, as they had done

[1] *Symposium*, 202 f.

the giants, then there would be an end of the sacrifices and worship which men offered; but, on the other hand, the gods could not suffer their insolence to be unrestrained. At last, after a good deal of reflection, Zeus discovered a way. He said: I think I have a plan which will humble their pride and their manners; men shall continue to exist, but I will cut them in two and then their strength will be diminished and their numbers increased; this will have the advantage of making them more profitable to us. They shall walk upright on two legs, and if they continue insolent and will not be quiet, I will split them again and they shall hop about on a single leg.' He spoke and cut men in two, like a sorb-apple which is halved for pickling, or as you might divide an egg with a hair; and as he cut them one after another, he told Apollo to give the face and the half of the neck a turn in order that the man might contemplate the section of himself; he would thus learn a lesson of humility.

Each of us when separated has one side only, like a flat fish, and is but the indenture of a man, and he is always looking for his other half. And when one meets with his other half, the actual half of himself, the pair are lost in an amazement of love and friendship and intimacy, and one will not be out of the other's sight, as I may say, even for a moment: these are the people who pass their whole lives together; yet they could not explain what they want from one another. For the intense yearning which each of them has towards the other does not appear to be the desire of sexual intercourse, but of something else which the soul of either evidently desires and cannot tell, and of which she has only a dark and doubtful presentiment. Suppose Hephaestus, with his instruments, to come to the pair who are lying side by side, and to say to them, 'What do you people want of one another?' they would be unable to explain. And suppose further, that when he saw their perplexity he said: 'Do you desire to be wholly one; always day and night to be in one another's company? for if this is what you desire, I am ready to weld you into one and let you grow together, so that you shall become one instead of two, and, while you live, live your life together as if you were a single man, and after your death in the world below still be one departed soul instead of two—I ask whether this is what you passionately desire, and whether you are satisfied to attain this?'—there is not a man of them who when he heard the proposal would not acknowledge that this meeting and melting into one another, this becoming one instead of two, was the very expression of his ancient need. And the reason is that human nature was originally one and we were a whole, and the desire and pursuit of the whole is called love. There was a time, I say, when we were one, but now because of the wickedness of mankind God has dispersed us, as the Arcadians were dispersed into villages by the Lacedaemonians. And if we are not obedient to the gods, there is a danger that we shall be split up again and go about in basso-relievo, like the profile figures with only half a nose which are sculptured on monuments, or like tallies. So let us exhort all men to reverence the gods, that we may avoid evil, and obtain the good, of which Love is our lord and minister; and let no one oppose him—the gods hate those who oppose him. For if we are friends of God and at peace with him we shall find our own true loves, which rarely happens in this world at present.[1]

[1] *Symposium*, 189 f.

CHAPTER III

RELIGION

The Creation of the World

Tim. Let me tell you then why the Creator made this world. He was good, and the good can never have any jealousy of anything. And because he was free from jealousy, he desired all things to be as like himself as they could be. This is in the truest sense the origin of creation and of the world, as we shall do well in believing on the testimony of wise men: God desired that all things should be good and nothing bad, so far as this was attainable. So finding all that is visible not at rest, but in irregular and disorderly movement, he brought order out of disorder, considering that this was in every way better than the other. Now the work of Him who is supremely the best could never be or have been other than most beautiful; and the creator, reflecting on the things which are by nature visible, found that taking things as a whole, no unintelligent creature was more beautiful than the intelligent, and that intelligence could not be present in anything which was devoid of soul. For this reason, when he was framing the universe, he put intelligence in soul, and soul in body, that he might be the creator of a work which was by nature most beautiful and best. So the most likely hypothesis is that the world became a living creature truly endowed with soul and intelligence by the providence of God.[1]

[1] *Timaeus*, 29 f.

God and Man

Who are the Gods, and what is their nature? Must they not be at least rulers who have to order unceasingly the whole heaven? And to what earthly rulers can they be compared, or who to them? How in the less can we find an image of the greater? Perhaps they might be compared to the generals of armies, or to doctors providing against the diseases which make war upon the body, or to farmers observing anxiously the effects of the seasons on the growth of plants; or perhaps to shepherds of flocks. For as we acknowledge the world to be full of much good and also of much evil, and of more evil than good, there is, we assert, an immortal conflict going on which requires wonderful vigilance; and in that conflict the Gods and demigods are our allies, and we are their property. Injustice and insolence and folly are the destruction of us, and justice and temperance and wisdom are our salvation; and the home of these virtues is in the life of the Gods, although some vestige of them may occasionally be discerned among mankind.[1]

Ath. God, as the old tradition declares, holding in His hand the beginning, middle, and end of all that is, travels according to His nature in a straight line towards the accomplishment of His end. Justice always accompanies Him, and punishes those who fall short of the divine law. Those who wish to be happy cling to justice and follow in her train with all humility and order; but he who is lifted up with pride, or elated by wealth or rank,

[1] *Laws*, 905 f.

or beauty, who is young and foolish, and has a soul hot with insolence, and thinks that he has no need of any guide or ruler, but is able himself to be the guide of others, he, I say, is forsaken by God; and in his loneliness he takes to him others like himself, throwing everything into wild confusion, and many think that he is a great man, but in a short time he pays a penalty which justice cannot but approve, and is utterly destroyed, and his family and city with him. So, seeing that the world is thus ordered, what should a wise man do or think, or not do or think?

Cle. Every man ought to make up his mind that he will be one of the followers of God; there can be no doubt of that.

Ath. Then what life is agreeable to God, and becoming in His followers? One only, expressed once for all in the old saying that 'like agrees with like, measure with measure', but things which have no measure agree neither with themselves nor with the things which have. Now God ought to be to us the measure of all things, and not man,[1] as men commonly say: the words are far more true of Him. And he who would be dear to God must, as far as is possible, be like Him and such as He is. So the right-minded man is the friend of God, for he is like Him; and the wrong-minded and unjust man is unlike Him, and different from Him. This is universally true, and from it follows the noblest and truest of all rules—that for the good man to offer sacrifice to the Gods, and hold communion with them through prayers and offerings

[1] The allusion to the saying of the sophist Protagoras: Man is the measure of all things.'

and every kind of service, is the noblest and best of all things, and also the most conducive to true happiness.[1]

The materialist view. The materialist argues that matter alone has a real existence, and that everything is ultimately derived from it. Religion, morals, political ideals, law, and art are merely human inventions, and have no basis in nature; they are what we should call epiphenomena, and what Plato calls 'art' (in distinction from nature). The materialist view could not be more ruthlessly put: note how Plato, quite logically on materialist premises, rejects art and music as baseless trifles.

Ath. They say that the greatest and most beautiful things are the work of nature and of chance, the lesser ones of art, which takes from the hand of nature her great and primal creations and moulds and fashions all those lesser works which are generally termed artificial.

Cle. What do you mean?

Ath. I will explain. The materialists say that fire and water, and earth and air, owe their existence to nature or chance, and not to art; and that the bodies which come next in order,—earth, sun, moon, stars,—have been created by means of these absolutely soulless agents, which drifted together casually, following their own natural laws, and produced all the heavens and their contents, and, in due course, animals and plants. Neither mind, nor God had anything to do with it: it was the work of nature and chance alone. Art, the subsequent and late-born product of these causes, herself as perishable as her creators, has since

[1] *Laws*, 716 f.

produced certain toys, with little real substance in them, such as music and painting and their companion arts. The only arts which produce anything of serious value are those which co-operate with nature, such, for example, as medicine, and husbandry, and gymnastic. Politics, they say, has something in common with nature, but more with art; while legislation is entirely a work of art, and is based on assumptions which are not true. As for the Gods, these people would say that they have no natural or real existence, but that they are the creations of art and of convention, and vary from place to place, according to the convention which established them. They say that there is no such thing as natural justice: but men are always disputing about justice and altering it; and the alterations which are made by art and by law have no basis in nature, but are valid only for the moment and at the time at which they are made.—These, my friends, are the sayings of men whom the young take to be wise—poets and prose writers, who say that the highest right is might. Hence our epidemics of youthful irreligion, under the idea that the Gods are not such as the law tells us to believe; hence too political factions, which come from these philosophers inviting men to lead 'the true natural life', which in fact means dominating their neighbours, and not, as they put it, 'living in the servitude to them which convention approves'.

Cle. What a dreadful picture, Stranger, have you given, and how great is the injury which is thus inflicted on young men to the ruin both of states and families![1]

[1] *Laws*, 889. Here and elsewhere in the *Laws* I have

To the materialist Plato replies that the soul is as 'natural' as matter, and that it, not matter, is the original and directing force in the universe—'a piece of divinity in us that was before the elements and owes no homage to the sun'.

Ath. Does not he who talks in this way conceive fire and water and earth and air to be the first elements of all things? these he calls nature, and out of these he supposes the soul to be formed afterwards. He affirms that which is the first cause of all things, to be not first, but last, and that which is last to be first, and this is the cause of his mistake about the true nature of the Gods. Nearly all of these thinkers seem to have failed to realize the nature and power of the soul, and especially her origin: they do not know that she is among the first of things, and before all bodies, and is the chief author of their changes and transpositions. And if this is true, and if soul is prior to body, must not the things which are akin to the soul be of necessity prior to those which belong to the body? But, if so, thought and attention and mind and art and law will be prior to hard and soft and heavy and light; and the great and primal works and actions will be those of art; they will be the first, and after them will come nature and works of nature, which, however, is a wrong term for men to apply to them; these will be secondary, and have their origin in art and mind.

Cle. But why is the word 'nature' wrong?

Ath. Because those who use the term mean to

borrowed some phrases from Prof. A. E. Taylor's translation.

say that nature is the first creative power; but if the soul turn out to be the primal element, and not fire or air, then in the truest sense and beyond other things the soul may be said to exist by nature; and this would be true if you proved that the soul is older than the body, but not otherwise.[1]

Plato's Answer to the Youthful Atheist

Our address to these lost and perverted natures should not be passionate; let us suppose ourselves to select some one of them, and gently reason with him, quenching our anger:—My son, we will say to him, you are young, and the advance of time will make you reverse many of the opinions which you now hold. Wait awhile, and do not attempt to judge at present of the highest issues; and the highest issue is the one which you now think trivial—to have the right view of the Gods and so to live well or ill. And in the first place let me indicate to you one point of great importance, about which I cannot be deceived:—You and your friends are not the first who have held this opinion about the Gods. There have always been persons more or less numerous who have had the same disease. I have known many of them, and can tell you, that no one who had adopted in youth the view, that the Gods do not exist, ever continued to hold it until he was old; the two other notions certainly do continue in some cases, but not in many; the notion, I mean, that the Gods exist, but pay no attention to human beings, and the other notion that they do pay attention, but are easily propitiated with sacrifices and prayers.

[1] *Laws*, 891 f.

If you will take my advice, you will wait for the clear belief in these matters which will come to you, reviewing them to see whether the truth lies here or there, and seeking guidance from others. In the meantime take care that you do not offend against the Gods.[1]

The Right Attitude to Religion

I feel myself (and I daresay that you have the same feeling) how hard and indeed impossible is the attainment of any certainty about questions such as these in the present life. And yet I should regard a man as a coward who did not test what is said about them to the uttermost, or whose heart failed him before he had examined them on every side. For he should persevere until he has achieved one of two things: either he should discover the truth about them for himself, or learn it from others: or, if this be impossible, I would have him take the best and most irrefragable of human theories, and let this be the raft upon which he sails through life—not without risk, as I admit, if he cannot find some word of God which will more surely and safely carry him.[2]

Religion in the State

Next we have to institute festivals and make laws about them, and to determine what sacrifices will be for the good of the city, and to what Gods they shall be offered; here we shall need the help of the Delphian oracle; but when they shall be offered, and how often, may be partly regulated by us. We will first determine the number; and let

[1] *Laws*, 888. [2] *Phaedo*, 85.

the whole number be 365—one for every day,—so that one magistrate at least will sacrifice daily to some God or demi-god on behalf of the city, and the citizens, and their possessions.[1]

The Prayer of Socrates

Beloved Pan, and all ye other gods who haunt this place, give me beauty in the inward soul; and may the outward and inward man be at one. May I reckon wisdom wealth, and may I have such a quantity of gold as a temperate man and he only can bear and carry.—Anything more? This prayer, I think, is enough for me.[2]

[1] *Laws*, 828.
[2] *Phaedrus*, 279.

CHAPTER IV

POLITICS: IDEALS AND REALITIES

Plato's political doctrines do not float in the air, but are firmly founded on his view of the ideal life for man. Having determined what the good life should be, he asks in what kind of state it can best be lived.

The Ideal State

Now good things are of two kinds, human and divine, and the human depend upon the divine; the state which attains the greater, at the same time acquires the less; if it fails to attain the greater, it is deprived of both. Of lesser goods the first is health, the second beauty, the third strength, including swiftness in running and in all other bodily movements, and the fourth is wealth, not blind, but keen of sight, and guided by wisdom. Among heavenly goods the first and foremost is wisdom; second right-mindedness allied with insight; third, and resulting from the union of these two with courage, is justice, and fourth in the scale of virtue is courage. All these naturally take precedence of the lesser goods, and this is the order in which the statesman must rank them. The ordinances which he prescribes to his citizens will be determined by these—the human looking to the divine, and the divine looking to their leader Reason.[1]

A state which would be secure and happy, as far as the nature of man allows, must and ought to

[1] *Laws*, 631.

distribute honour and dishonour in the right way. And the right way is to place the qualities of the soul first and highest in the scale, always assuming right-mindedness to be the condition of them; and to assign the second place to the goods of the body; and the third place to money and property. And if any statesman or state departs from this rule by giving money the place of honour, or in any way preferring that which is really last, may we not say, that he or the state is untrue both to religion and to statesmanship?[1]

The Greatness and Decline of Atlantis (*an Imaginary State*)

Such was the vast power which the god settled in the lost island of Atlantis. For many generations, as long as the divine nature lasted in them, they were obedient to the laws, and well-disposed towards the god, whose seed they were; for they had true and in every way great spirits, uniting gentleness with wisdom in the various fortunes of life, and in their intercourse with one another. They despised everything but virtue, caring little for their present state of life, and thinking lightly of the possession of gold and other property, which seemed only a burden to them; they were not intoxicated by luxury; nor did wealth deprive them of their self-control; but they were sober, and saw clearly that all these things are increased by virtue and mutual friendly feeling, while by too great regard and respect for them, they are lost and friendly relations with them. By such reflections and by the continuance in them of a divine

[1] *Laws*, 697.

nature, the qualities which we have described grew and increased among them; but when the divine element began to fade away, and became diluted too often and too much with the mortal admixture, and the human nature got the upper hand, they were carried away by their prosperity and went wrong, and to any clear-seeing eye grew visibly debased, for they were losing the fairest of their precious gifts; though to those who had no eye to see the true happiness, they appeared glorious and blessed at the very time when they were full of avarice and unrighteous power.[1]

How to save the World

Until philosophers are kings, or the kings and princes of this world have the spirit and power of philosophy, and political greatness and wisdom meet in one, and those commoner natures who pursue either to the exclusion of the other are compelled to stand aside, cities will never have rest from their evils,—no, nor the human race, as I believe,—and then only will this our State have a possibility of life and behold the light of day.[2]

If Plato holds this view, it is not that he is unaware of the popular view of philosophy and philosophers. The speaker is an Athenian politician, Callicles. (For other views of Callicles see p. 162.)

Philosophy, Socrates, if pursued in moderation and at the proper age, is a graceful accomplishment, but too much philosophy is the ruin of human life. Even if a man has good parts, still, if he carries philosophy into later life, he is

[1] *Critias*, 121 f. [2] *Republic*, 473.

necessarily ignorant of all the knowledge which is necessary if you wish to be a gentleman or a distinguished man; he knows nothing of the laws of the State, or of the language which ought to be used in the dealings of man with man, whether private or public, and he is utterly ignorant of the pleasures and desires of mankind and of human character in general. People of this sort, when they go into politics or business, are as ridiculous as I imagine the politicians to be, when they make their appearance in the arena of philosophy. For, as Euripides says,

> 'Every man shines in, and pursues, and devotes the greatest portion of the day, to that in which he most excels,'[1]

but anything in which he is inferior, he avoids and depreciates, and praises the opposite from partiality to himself, and because he thinks that this is a way to commend himself. The true principle is to unite them. Philosophy, as a part of education, is an excellent thing, and there is no disgrace to a man while he is young in pursuing such a study; but when he is more advanced in years, the thing becomes ridiculous, and gives me the same sort of feeling as I have about persons who lisp and imitate children. I love to see a little child, who is not of an age to speak plainly, lisping at his play; there is an appearance of grace and freedom in his utterance, which is natural to his childish years. But when I hear some small creature carefully articulating its words, it sounds disagreeable, and annoys my ears: there is something vulgar about

[1] *Antiope*, fragm. 20.

it. So when I hear a man lisping, or see him playing like a child, it strikes me as ridiculous and unmanly—he ought to be whipped. I have the same feeling about students of philosophy; when I see a young man occupied with it, his studies seem to me to be in character, and suitable to a man of a liberal education, and I regard a man who neglects philosophy as inferior—the sort of person who will never aspire to anything great or noble. But if I see him continuing the study in later life, and not leaving off, I should like to beat him, Socrates; for, as I was saying, a man like that, even though he has good natural parts, becomes effeminate. He flies from the centres of the city's life, in which, as the poet says, men win eminence; he creeps into a corner for the rest of his life, and talks in a whisper with three or four admiring youths, but never speaks out as a man should.[1]

Plato's Idea of a Philosopher

The essence of the philosopher is that he has a true vision of reality: Plato here suggests how this will affect his character as a man and a politician. It is Plato's merit to have seen that the thinker can be a man of action and that the man of action ought to be a thinker. There are examples of his philosopher-kings in history—Marcus Aurelius in the ancient world, Masaryk in recent times. The latter compares favourably with other contemporary statesmen.

Are not those who are absolutely destitute of the knowledge of things as they really are, and who have in their souls no clear pattern, and are

[1] *Gorgias*, 484 f.

unable like a painter to look at the absolute truth, and continually refer to it, and by their perfect vision of the other world to establish ideals of beauty, goodness, and justice on earth or, if established, to guard and preserve them—are not such persons, I ask, simply blind? And shall they be our guardians[1] when there are others who, besides being their equals in experience and falling short of them in no particular of virtue, also know the very truth of each thing? Suppose then that we determine how far they can combine both qualifications. In the first place we must ascertain what the philosophic nature is, and, when we have done so, then, if I am not mistaken, we shall also acknowledge that such a union of qualities is possible, and that those in whom they are united, and those only, should be rulers in the State.

Let us suppose that philosophical minds always love that kind of knowledge which reveals to them the eternal realities. And further, let us agree that they are lovers of reality as a whole: there is no part whether greater or less, or more or less honourable, which they are willing to renounce; here they are like lovers or ambitious men. And if they are to be what we were describing there is another quality which they should also possess—truthfulness: they will never intentionally admit into their mind falsehood, which is their detestation, and they will love the truth. And is there anything more akin to wisdom than truth? Can the same nature be a lover of wisdom and a lover of falsehood? If not, the true lover of learning

[1] The term Plato uses for his governing class.

must from his earliest youth, as far as in him lies, desire all truth?

But then, as we know by experience, if a man's desires set strongly in one direction, they will be weaker in others—they will be like a stream which has been drawn off into another channel; and a man whose desires are drawn towards knowledge in every form will be absorbed in the pleasures of the soul, and will hardly feel bodily pleasure—I mean, if he be a true philosopher and not a sham one. He is sure to be temperate, and the reverse of covetous; for the motives which make another man anxious to have and to spend, have no place in his character.

Another criterion of the philosophical nature has also to be considered. There should be no secret corner of illiberality in it; nothing can be more antagonistic than meanness to a soul which is ever longing after the whole of things both divine and human. And how can one who has greatness of mind and is the spectator of all time and all existence, think much of human life, or regard death as terrible? So cowardice and meanness are remote from true philosophy.

Or again: can one who is harmoniously constituted, who is not covetous or mean, or a boaster, or a coward—can he, I say, ever be unjust or hard in his dealings?[1]

He, whose mind is fixed upon Reality, has surely no time to look down upon the affairs of earth, or to be filled with malice and envy, in contention with men; his eye always directed towards a fixed

[1] *Republic*, 484 f.

and immutable world, where nothing does or suffers wrong but all moves in order at the command of Reason; this world he imitates, and to it he will, as far as he can, conform himself. A man cannot help imitating that with which he lives in admiring communion: and the philosopher, in his communion with the divine order, becomes orderly and divine, as far as the nature of man allows; but like every one else, he will have his enemies. And if he is forced to model not only himself, but human nature generally, whether in States or individuals, by that which he beholds in the other world, will he, think you, be an unskilful artist of justice, temperance, and every civil virtue? And if the world perceives that what we are saying about him is the truth, will they be angry with philosophy? Will they disbelieve us, when we tell them that no State can be happy which is not designed by artists who imitate the heavenly pattern?[1]

Our rulers must be lovers of their country, tried by the test of pleasures and pains, and neither in hardships, nor in dangers, nor at any other critical moment must they lose their patriotism—those who fail in the test must be rejected, but those who always emerge unstained, like gold tried in the fire, shall be made rulers, and receive honours and rewards in life and after death. Previously I shrank from making the bold statement which I shall now make—that the perfect guardian must be a philosopher. And do not suppose that there will be many of them; for the gifts which were

[1] *Republic*, 500.

deemed by us to be essential rarely grow together; they are mostly found in shreds and patches. Quick intelligence, memory, sagacity, cleverness, and similar qualities, do not often grow together, and persons who possess them and are at the same time high-spirited and magnanimous are not so constituted by nature as to live an orderly and peaceful and settled life. Their vivacity drives them this way and that, and they lose their stability. On the other hand, those steadfast natures which can better be depended upon, which in a battle are impregnable to fear and immovable, are equally immovable when there is anything to be learned; they are always in a torpid state, and are apt to yawn and go to sleep over any intellectual toil. And yet we were saying that both qualities were necessary in those to whom the higher education is to be imparted, and who are to share in any office or command. But such persons are rare. So the future ruler must not only be tested in those labours and dangers and pleasures which we mentioned before, but there is another kind of probation which we did not mention—he must be exercised also in many kinds of knowledge, to see whether the soul will be able to endure the highest of all, or will faint under them, as in any other studies and exercises.[1]

As this passage indicates, Plato's 'philosopher-kings' are much more than mere thinkers. Besides an elaborate education in science and philosophy, they have rigorous physical training and serve in the army. Their character is as severely tested as their intellect.

[1] *Republic*, 503 f.

The final stage in their education is the study of the 'Idea of the Good' (*p.* 47), *here called 'the Absolute Good'; because the final and indispensable qualification for a statesman is that he should have the right view of the world and of life.*

When our rulers have reached fifty years of age, then let those who have won through and have excelled in every sphere of action and knowledge be introduced at last to their final task: the time has now arrived at which they must raise the eye of the soul to the universal light which lightens all things, and behold the Absolute Good; for that is the pattern according to which they are to order the State and the lives of individuals, and the remainder of their own lives too; making philosophy their chief pursuit, but, when their turn comes, toiling also at politics and ruling for the public good, not as though they were performing some heroic action, but simply as a matter of duty; and when they have brought up in each generation others like themselves and left them in their place to be governors of the State, then they will depart to the Islands of the Blest and there dwell.[1]

Doubtful if even the best training can produce the rulers he desires, Plato proposes to make them disinterested by closing to them the two inlets through which private interest creeps in—property and family life. His ruling class are to have wives and possessions in common. So the last temptation to selfishness will be taken away.

[1] *Republic*, 540.

With the following description of the ideal of national unity no one will quarrel, but few will accept the practical conclusion, and Plato, though he puts forward communism (for the ruling class only) as an ideal, thought it impracticable. His communism is an anticipation of the ideal of the religious orders, and has no relation to modern communism.

Can there be any greater evil in a State than discord and distraction and plurality where unity ought to reign? or any greater good than the bond of unity? There is unity where there is community of pleasures and pains—where all the citizens are glad or grieved on the same occasions of joy and sorrow; and where there is no common but only private feeling a State is disorganized—when one half of its people are delighted and the other plunged in grief at the same events happening to the city or the citizens. Such differences commonly originate in a disagreement about the use of the terms 'mine' and 'not mine', 'his' and 'not his', and the best-ordered State is that in which the greatest number of persons apply the terms 'mine' and 'not mine' in the same way to the same thing. So the best State is that which most closely resembles the individual human being. Take our body for example: when but a finger of one of us is hurt, the whole frame, drawn towards the soul as a centre and forming one kingdom under its ruling power, feels the hurt and sympathizes all together with the part affected, and we say that the man has a pain in his finger; and the same expression is used about any other part of the body, which has a sensation of pain at suffering or of pleasure at the alleviation of suffering. Very true, he replied; and I agree with you that in the best-ordered State there is the nearest approach to this common feeling which you describe. Then when any one of the citizens experiences any good or evil, the whole State will make his case their own, and will either rejoice or sorrow with him? Yes, he said, that is what will happen in a well-ordered State.[1]

Our citizens will have a common interest; each will call that interest 'mine'; so they will share each other's pleasures and pains. And the reason of this, over and above the general constitution of the State, will be that the governing class will have wives and children in common. And this unity of feeling we admitted to be the greatest good, as was implied in our own comparison of a well-ordered State to the relation of the body and the members, when affected by pleasure or pain? So the community of wives and children among our citizens is clearly the source of the greatest good to the State. And this agrees with the other principle which we were affirming—that the governing class were not to have houses or lands or any other property; their pay was to be their food, which they were to receive from the other citizens, and they were to have no private expenses; for we intended them to preserve their true character of guardians. Both the community of property and the community of families tend to make them more truly guardians; they will not tear the city in pieces by differing about 'mine' and 'not mine';

[1] *Republic*, 462.

each man dragging any acquisition which he has made into a separate house of his own, where he has a separate wife and children and private pleasures and pains; but all will be affected as far as may be by the same pleasures and pains because they are all of one opinion about what is near and dear to them, and therefore they all tend towards a common end. And as they have nothing but their persons which they can call their own, lawsuits and complaints will have no existence among them; they will be delivered from all those quarrels of which money or children or relations are the occasion. And as the governing classes will never quarrel among themselves there will be no danger of the rest of the city being divided either against them or against one another. I hardly like even to mention petty meannesses of which they will be set free, for they are beneath notice: such, for example, as the flattery of the rich by the poor, and all the pains and pangs which men experience in bringing up a family, and in finding money to buy necessaries for their household, borrowing and then repudiating, getting how they can, and giving the money into the hands of women and slaves to keep—the many evils of so many kinds which people suffer in this way are mean enough and obvious enough, and not worth speaking of. They will escape all these evils, and their life will be blessed as the life of Olympic victors and even more blessed. For the victory which they have won is the salvation of the whole State; and the crown with which they and their children are crowned is the fullness of all that life needs; they receive honours from the hands of their country while living, and after death have an honourable burial.[1]

The Test of a Statesman

Socrates is speaking to a contemporary politician, Callicles.

Soc. And now, my friend, as you are already beginning to be a prominent politician, and are rebuking and reproaching me for not being one, suppose that we ask a few questions of one another. Tell me, then, Callicles, how about making any of the citizens better? Was there ever a man who was once vicious, or unjust, or intemperate, or foolish, and became by the help of Callicles good and noble? Was there ever such a man, whether citizen or stranger, slave or freeman? Tell me, Callicles, if a person were to ask these questions of you, what would you answer? Whom would you say that you had improved by your conversation? You may have done such acts in private life, before you came forward in public. Why will you not answer?

Cal. You are contentious, Socrates.

Soc. No, I ask you, not from a love of contention, but because I really want to know what you think that political life in Athens should be like—whether, when you come to the administration of it, you have any other aim but the improvement of the citizens? Have we not already admitted many times over that such is the duty of a public man?[2]

[1] *Republic*, 464.
[2] *Gorgias*, 515.

Taking this test of a statesman, Socrates criticizes Pericles, Miltiades, and other famous Athenian politicians.

Cal. But surely, Socrates, no living man ever came near any one of them in his performances.

Soc. O, my dear friend, I say nothing against them regarded as the serving-men of the State; and I do think that they were certainly more serviceable than those who are living now, and better able to gratify the wishes of the State; but as to transforming those desires and not allowing them to have their way, and using the powers which they had, whether of persuasion or of force, in the improvement of their fellow-citizens, which is the prime object of the truly good citizen, I do not see that in these respects they were a whit superior to our present statesmen, although I do admit that they were more clever at providing ships and fortifications and docks, and all that.[1]

The statesman ought to be like the trainer who brings the human body into good condition, not like the cook or confectioner who gratifies its appetites.

You come repeating, Has not the State had good and noble citizens? and when I ask you who they are, you reply, seemingly quite in earnest, as if I had asked, Who are or have been good athletic trainers?—and you had replied, Thearion, the baker, Mithoecus, who wrote the Sicilian cookery-book, Sarambus, the vintner: these are ministers to the body, first-rate in their art; for the first makes admirable bread, the second excellent dishes, and

[1] *Gorgias*, 517.

the third capital wine;—to me these appear to be the exact parallel of the statesmen whom you mention. Now you would not be altogether pleased if I said to you, My friend, you know nothing of gymnastics; those of whom you are speaking to me are only the ministers and purveyors of luxury, who have no good or exalted notions of their art, and may very likely be filling and fattening men's bodies and gaining their approval, although the result is that they lose their original flesh in the long run, and become thinner than they were before; and yet they, in their simplicity, will not attribute their diseases and loss of flesh to their entertainers; but when in after years the unhealthy surfeit brings the attendant penalty of disease, he who happens to be near them at the time, and offers them advice, is accused and blamed by them, and if they could they would do him some harm; while they proceed to eulogize the men who have been the real authors of the mischief. And that, Callicles, is just what you are now doing. You praise the men who feasted the citizens and satisfied their desires, and people say that they have made the city great, not seeing that the swollen and ulcerated condition of the State is to be attributed to these elder statesmen; for they have filled the city full of harbours and docks and forts and revenues and all that, and have left no room for justice and temperance. And when the crisis of the disorder comes, the people will blame the advisers of the hour, and applaud Themistocles and Cimon and Pericles, who are the real authors of their calamities.[1]

[1] *Gorgias*, 518.

This is a novel and astonishing way of regarding national heroes. (To appreciate Plato's attitude, write Marlborough for Miltiades and — perhaps — Lloyd George for Pericles.) Yet it may be that statesmen will finally be judged by the standards of Plato. The moral currency of politics has been debased by the popular admiration for men like Frederick the Great, Bismarck, and Napoleon, whose policy has 'in after years brought the attendant penalty of disease' to their nations.

The reason why true statesmen are rare is the corrupting influence of the public.

Do you really think, as people so often say, that our youth are corrupted by Sophists, or that private teachers of the art corrupt them in any degree worth speaking of? Are not the public who say these things the greatest of all Sophists? And do they not educate to perfection young and old, men and women alike, and fashion them after their own hearts? When they meet together, and the world sits down at an assembly, or in a court of law, or a theatre, or a camp, or in any other popular resort, and there is a great uproar, and they praise some things which are being said or done, and blame other things, both with equal exaggeration, shouting and clapping their hands, and the echo of the rocks and the place in which they are assembled redoubles the sound of the praise or blame—at such a time will not a young man's heart, as they say, leap within him? Will any private training enable him to stand firm against the overwhelming flood of popular opinion? or will he be carried away by the stream? Will he not have the notions of good and evil which the public in general have—he will do as they do, and as they are, such will he be?[1]

We have no 'Sophists', but perhaps there are journalists whose attitude to the public is described in the following passage.

Those mercenary individuals, whom the masses call Sophists and whom they regard as their enemies, do, in fact, teach nothing but the opinion of the crowd, when it meets *en masse*. This is their wisdom. I might compare them to a man who studied the tempers and desires of a mighty strong beast who is fed by him—he would learn how to approach and handle him, also at what times and from what causes he is dangerous or the reverse, and what is the meaning of his several cries, and what noises made by other people infuriate him; and you may suppose further, that when, by continually attending upon him, he has become a master of all this, he calls his knowledge wisdom, and turns it into a system or art, which he proceeds to teach, although he has no real notion of what he means by the principles or passions of which he is speaking. He calls this honourable and that dishonourable, or good or evil, or just or unjust, all in accordance with the tastes and tempers of the great brute. Good he pronounces to be that in which the beast delights and evil to be that which it dislikes.[2]

The Philosopher in a Corrupt State

The worthy disciples of philosophy will be but a small remnant: perhaps some noble and well-educated person, detained by exile in her service, who in the absence of corrupting influences remains

[1] *Republic*, 492. [2] Ibid., 493.

devoted to her; or some lofty soul born in a mean city, the politics of which he despises and neglects; and there may be a gifted few who leave some profession which they justly despise, and come to her;—or possibly there are some who are restrained by our friend Theages' bridle; for everything in the life of Theages conspired to divert him from philosophy; but ill-health kept him away from politics. Those who belong to this small class have tasted how sweet and blessed a possession philosophy is, and have also seen enough of the madness of the multitude; and they know that no politician is honest, nor is there any champion of justice at whose side they may fight and be saved. Such an one may be compared to a man who has fallen among wild beasts—he will not join in the wickedness of his fellows, but neither is he able singly to resist all their fierce natures, and so seeing that he would be of no use to the State or to his friends, and reflecting that he would have to throw away his life without doing any good either to himself or others, he holds his peace, and goes his own way. He is like one who, in the storm of dust and sleet which the driving wind hurries along, retires under the shelter of a wall; and seeing the rest of the world full of wickedness, he is content, if only he can live his own life and be pure from evil or unrighteousness, and depart in peace and good-will, with bright hopes.[1]

A fable of the development of civilization and of the qualities necessary for the preservation of society.

Once upon a time there were gods only, and no

[1] *Republic*, 496.

mortal creatures. But when the time came that these also should be created, the gods fashioned them in the interior of the earth out of earth and fire and various mixtures of both elements; and when they were about to bring them into the light of day, they ordered Prometheus and Epimetheus to equip them, and to distribute to them severally their proper qualities. Epimetheus said to Prometheus: 'Let me distribute, and do you inspect.' This was agreed, and Epimetheus made the distribution. There were some to whom he gave strength without swiftness, while he equipped the weaker with swiftness; some he armed, and others he left unarmed; and devised for the latter some other means of preservation, making some large, and having their size as a protection, and others small, whose nature was to fly in the air or burrow in the ground; this was to be their way of escape. Thus did he compensate them, with the view of preventing any race from becoming extinct. And when he had provided against their destruction by one another, he contrived also a means of protecting them against the seasons of heaven; clothing them with close hair and thick skins sufficient to defend them against the winter cold and able to resist the summer heat, so that they might have a natural bed of their own when they wanted to rest; also he furnished them with hoofs and hair and hard and callous skins under their feet. Then he gave them varieties of food,—herb of the soil to some, to others fruits of trees, and to others roots, and to some again he gave other animals as food. And some he made to have few young ones, while those who were their prey were very prolific; and in this manner the species was preserved. Thus did Epimetheus, who, not being very wise, forgot that he had distributed among the brute animals all the qualities which he had to give—and when he came to man, who was still unprovided, he was terribly perplexed. Now while he was in this perplexity, Prometheus came to inspect the distribution, and he found that the other animals were suitably furnished, but that man alone was naked and shoeless, and had neither bed nor arms of defence. The appointed hour was approaching when man in his turn was to go forth into the light of day; and Prometheus, not knowing how he could devise his salvation, stole the mechanical arts of Hephaestus and Athene,[1] and fire with them (they could neither have been acquired nor used without fire), and gave them to man. Thus man had the wisdom necessary to the support of life, but political wisdom he had not; for that was in the keeping of Zeus, and the power of Prometheus did not extend to entering into the citadel of heaven, where Zeus dwelt, guarded too by terrible sentinels; but he did enter by stealth into the common workshop of Athene and Hephaestus, in which they used to practise their favourite arts, and carried off Hephaestus' art of working by fire, and also the art of Athene, and gave them to man. And in this way man was supplied with the means of life.

Now man, having a share of the divine attributes, was at first the only one of the animals who had any gods, because he alone was of their kindred; and he would raise altars and images of

[1] The art of working metals, and the textile art.

them. He was not long in inventing articulate speech and names; and he also constructed houses and clothes and shoes and beds, and drew sustenance from the earth. Thus provided, mankind at first lived dispersed, and there were no cities. But the consequence was that they were destroyed by wild beasts, for they were utterly weak in comparison of them, and their art was only sufficient to provide them with the means of life, and did not enable them to carry on war against the animals: food they had, but not as yet the art of government, of which the art of war is a part. After a while the desire of self-preservation gathered them into cities; but when they were gathered together, having no art of government, they treated one another unjustly, and were again in process of dispersion and destruction. Zeus feared that the entire race would be exterminated, and so he sent Hermes to them, bearing conscience[1] and justice to be the regulating principles of states and the ties which unite men in friendly relations. Hermes asked Zeus how he should impart justice and conscience among men:—Should he distribute them as technical skill is distributed; that is to say, to a favoured few only, one skilled individual having enough of medicine or of any other art for many unskilled ones? 'Shall this be the principle on which I am to distribute justice and conscience among men, or shall I give them to all?' 'To all,'

[1] The word here translated 'conscience' is αἰδώς. It is the instructive sense of decency and honour that prevents men doing certain things, which perhaps law or even justice would not forbid, but which are wrong. There is no profounder diagnosis of the ultimate political problem than is contained in this final passage of the fable.

said Zeus; 'I should like them all to have a share; for states cannot exist, if a few only share in the virtues, as in the arts. And further, make a law by my order, that he who is utterly without conscience and justice shall be put to death, for he is a disease in the state.'[1]

A fundamental (and often-forgotten) principle of politics.

Governments vary as the dispositions of men vary. Or do you suppose that political constitutions are made out of rocks or trees, and not out of the dispositions of their citizens which turn the scale and draw everything in their own direction?[2]

The Element of Chance in Politics

I was going to say that man never legislates; accidents of all sorts legislate for us in all sorts of ways. The violence of war and the hard necessity of poverty are constantly overturning governments and changing laws. And disease has often caused revolutions, when pestilences occur, or when there has been a succession of bad seasons continuing during many years. Any one who sees all this naturally rushes to the conclusion that no mortal legislates in anything, but that in human history chance is almost everything. And yet there is another thing which may be said with equal truth—that God governs all things, and that chance and opportunity co-operate with Him in the government of human affairs. But a third and more amenable element should be present—art.[3]

[1] *Protagoras*, 320 f. [2] *Republic*, 544.
[3] *Laws*, 709. By 'art' Plato means political science—human thought and skill.

The State and the Citizen

Socrates in prison, a day or two before his execution, is replying to a friend who urges him to escape.

Imagine that I am about to play truant (you may call the proceeding by any name which you like), and the laws and the government come and question me: 'Tell us, Socrates,' they say; 'what are you about? are you not going by an act of yours to overthrow us—the laws, and the whole state, as far as in you lies? Do you imagine that a state can subsist and not be overthrown, in which the decisions of law are impotent and set aside and trampled upon by individuals?' What will be our answer, Crito, to these and the like words? Shall we reply, 'Yes; but the state has injured us and sentenced us unjustly?' 'And was that our agreement with you?' the law would answer; 'or were you to abide by the sentence of the state?' And if I were to express my astonishment at their words, the law would probably add: 'Answer, Socrates, instead of opening your eyes—you are in the habit of asking and answering questions. Tell us,—What complaint have you to make against us which justifies you in attempting to destroy us and the state? In the first place did we not bring you into existence? Your father married your mother by our aid and begat you. Say whether you have any objection to urge against those of us who regulate marriage?' None, I should reply. 'Or against those of us who after birth regulate the upbringing and education of children, in which you also were trained? Were not the laws, which have the charge of education, right in commanding your father to train you in music and gymnastic?'[1] Right, I should reply. 'Well then, since you were brought into the world and brought up and educated by us, can you deny in the first place that you are our child and servant, as your fathers were before you? And if this is true you are not on equal terms with us; nor can you think that you have a right to do to us what we are doing to you. Would you have any right to strike or abuse or do any other harm to your father or your master if you had one, because you have been struck or abused by him, or received some other harm at his hands?—you would not say this? And because we think right to destroy you, do you think that you have any right to destroy us in return, and your country as far as in you lies? Will you, the professor of true virtue, pretend that you are justified in this? Has a philosopher like you failed to discover that our country is more to be valued and higher and holier far than mother or father or any ancestor, and more to be regarded in the eyes of the gods and of men of understanding? to be reverenced, and to be humoured in its anger, even more than a father, and either to be persuaded, or if not persuaded, to be obeyed? And when we are punished by her, whether with imprisonment or flogging, the punishment is to be endured in silence; and if she lead us to wounds or death in battle, we must comply—that is our duty; a man must not surrender or retreat or leave his rank, but whether in battle or in a court of law, or in any other place, he must do what his city and

[1] The two sides of Greek education. 'Music' includes reading, writing, literature, &c.

his country order him; or he must change their view of what is just: and if he may do no violence to his father or mother, much less may he do violence to his country.' What answer shall we make to this, Crito? Do the laws speak truly, or do they not? Then the laws will say: 'Consider, Socrates, if we are right in saying that in your present attempt you are going to do us an injury. Having brought you into the world, and educated you, and given you and every other citizen a share in every good which we had to give, we further proclaim to any Athenian by the liberty which we allow him, that if he does not like us when he has become of age and has seen the ways of the city, and made our acquaintance, he may go where he pleases and take his property with him. None of the laws will forbid him or interfere with him. Any one who does not like us and the city, and who wants to emigrate to a colony or to any other city, may go where he likes, and keep his property. But he who has experience of our ways of ordering justice and administering the state, and still remains, has entered into an implied contract that he will do as we command him. And he who disobeys us is, as we maintain, thrice wrong; first, because in disobeying us he is disobeying his parents; secondly, because we are the authors of his education; thirdly, because he has made an agreement with us duly to obey our commands; and he neither obeys them nor convinces us that our commands are unjust.

'Listen, then, Socrates, to us who have brought you up. Think not of life and children first, and of justice afterwards, but of justice first, that you may be justified before the rulers of the world below. For neither you nor any that belong to you will be happier or holier or juster in this life, or happier in another, if you do as Crito bids. Now you depart in innocence, a sufferer and not a doer of evil; a victim, not of the laws but of men. But if you go forth, returning evil for evil, and injury for injury, breaking the covenants and agreements which you have made with us, and wronging those whom you ought least of all to wrong, that is to say, yourself, your friends, your country, and us, we shall be angry with you while you live, and our brethren, the laws in the world below, will receive you as an enemy; for they will know that you have done your best to destroy us. Listen, then, to us and not to Crito.'

This, dear Crito, is the voice which I seem to hear murmuring in my ears, like the sound of the flute in the ears of the mystic; that voice, I say, is humming in my ears, and prevents me from hearing any other. And I know that anything more which you may say will be vain. Yet speak, if you have anything to say.

Cr. I have nothing to say, Socrates.

Soc. Leave me, then, Crito, to fulfil the will of God, and to follow whither he leads.[1]

Some Types of State

1. *The Military State* (*Sparta or Crete in the ancient world, Prussia in the modern*).

The Cretan legislator[2] seems to me to have

[1] *Crito*, 50 f.

[2] Or, as we should say, the maker of the Cretan constitution.

thought the world foolish in not understanding that all men are always at war with one another. For what men in general term peace would be said by him to be only a name; in reality every city is in a natural state of war with every other, not indeed formally proclaimed, but unceasing. And if you look closely, you will find that this was the intention of the Cretan legislator; all institutions, private as well as public, were arranged by him with a view to war; in giving them he was under the impression that no possessions or institutions are of any value to him who is defeated in battle; for all the assets of the conquered pass into the hands of the conquerors.[1]

The Cause of the Fall of the Military State

You will remember, what I said at first, that a statesman and legislator ought to frame his ordinances with his eye on wisdom; while you were arguing that the good lawgiver ought to order everything with a view to war. And to this I replied that there were four virtues, but that upon your view one of them only was the aim of legislation; whereas you ought to legislate with a view to all virtue, and especially the virtue which comes first, and is the leader of all the rest—I mean wisdom and reason and judgment and the ardent aspirations which go with them. And now we are back at the same point, and I say once more, in jest if you like, or in earnest if you like, that the prayer of a fool is full of danger, and likely to end in the opposite of what he desires. And if you would rather take my words as serious, I am will-

[1] *Laws*, 625 f.

ing that you should; and you will find, I suspect, as I have said already, that not cowardice was the cause of the ruin of the Dorian kings and of their design, nor ignorance of military matters, either on the part of the rulers or of their subjects; but their misfortunes were due to their general degeneracy, and especially to their ignorance of the most important things in human life.[1]

2. *The Autocratic State.*

Like Carlyle, Plato sees the argument for the 'hero as king', but, unlike Carlyle, he sees the fatal objection to a government founded on this principle.

There is a tradition of the happy life of mankind in the days of effortless and spontaneous plenty. The reason for it is said to have been that Cronos[2] knew that no human nature invested with supreme power is able to order human affairs without becoming inflated with pride and injustice. This reflection led him to appoint demigods, who are of a higher and more divine race, to be the kings and rulers of our cities instead of men; he did as we do with flocks of sheep and other tame animals. For we do not appoint oxen to be the lords of oxen, or goats of goats; but we ourselves as a superior race rule over them. Similarly God, in His love of mankind, placed over us a superior race of spirits, and they with great ease and pleasure to themselves, and no less to us, watched over us and gave us peace and conscience and order and unfailing justice, and made the tribes of men happy

[1] Ibid., 688.

[2] The supreme god who preceded Zeus and ruled the golden age.

and united. And this tradition reminds us that cities of which some mortal man and not God is the ruler, have no escape from evils and toils. But we must do all that we can to imitate the life which is said to have existed in the days of Cronos, and we must obey the immortal element in ourselves, both in private and public life and regulate our states and homes by it, and give the name of law to the decree of reason. But if either an individual or an oligarchy or a democracy has a soul eager after pleasures and desires—wanting to be filled with them, yet retaining none of them, and perpetually afflicted with an endless and insatiable disorder; and this evil spirit having first trampled the laws under foot, becomes the master either of a state or of an individual,—then, as I was saying, salvation is hopeless.[1]

In no very long period of time, an autocrat, if he wishes, can change the manners of a state: he has only to go in the direction of virtue or of vice, whichever he prefers, he himself indicating by his example the lines of conduct, praising and rewarding some actions and rebuking others, and degrading those who disobey. The quickest and easiest way for a state to change its laws is through the leadership of its masters: such changes never have, and never will, come to pass in any other way. The real impossibility or difficulty is of another sort, and is rarely surmounted in the course of ages; but when once it is surmounted, every kind of blessing follows.

Of what are you speaking?

[1] *Laws*, 713 f.

The difficulty is to find a divine passion for rational and just institutions in any powerful forms of government, whether in a monarchy or an oligarchy of wealth or of birth. You might as well hope to reproduce the character of Nestor, who is said to have surpassed all men in eloquence, and even more in wisdom. This, however, according to tradition, was in the times of Troy; it has never occurred in our own; but if there is, has been, or ever shall be such a person, blessed is his life, and blessed are they who hear the wise words that flow from his lips. And this may be said of power in general: When the supreme power in man coincides with the greatest wisdom and temperance, then the best laws and the best constitution come into being; but in no other way.[1]

Men can never be made to believe that any one can be worthy of absolute authority, or be able and willing to rule in the spirit of virtue and knowledge and give every one his right and just due; they fancy that he will be a despot who will wrong and injure and kill any of us whom he wishes; for if there could be such a despot as we describe, they would acknowledge that we ought to be too glad to have him, and that he alone would be the happy ruler of a true and perfect State. But, as the State is not like a beehive, and has no natural head who is at once recognized to be the superior both in body and mind, mankind are obliged to combine to make laws, and try to approach as nearly as they can to the true form of government.[2]

[1] Ibid., 711.
[2] *Statesman*, 301.

The Effect of Autocracy on the Autocrat

If one ignores the law of proportion and gives too great power to anything, too large a sail to a vessel, too much food to the body, too much authority to the mind, everything is shipwrecked: the excess breaks out in the one case in disease, and in the other in injustice, the child of pride. I mean to say, my dear friends, that no human soul, in its youth and irresponsibility, will be able to sustain the temptation of arbitrary power—there is no one who will not, under such circumstances, become filled with folly, that worst of diseases, and be hated by his nearest and dearest friends: when this happens his kingdom is undermined, and all his power vanishes.[1]

3. *The Plutocratic State.*

This in Plato's view arises out of 'timocracy', whose guiding principle is 'honour'. Sparta was the typical timocracy of antiquity: and Plato would have regarded the rule of the landed-gentleman class in our country as timocratic. Timocracy, Plato thinks, tends to develop into 'oligarchy', which corresponds to unrestricted capitalism, with its sharp division between rich and poor.

The accumulation of gold in the treasury of private individuals is the ruin of timocracy; they invent illegal modes of expenditure; for what do they or their wives care about the law? And then one, seeing another grow rich, tries to rival him, and so the great mass of the citizens become lovers of money, and so they grow richer and richer, and the more they think of making a fortune the less

[1] *Laws*, 691.

they think of goodness; for when riches and goodness are placed together in the scales of the balance, the one always rises as the other falls. And in proportion as riches and rich men are honoured in the State, goodness and the good are dishonoured, and so at last, instead of the life of rivalry and glory, men become lovers of trade and money; they honour and look up to the rich man, and make a ruler of him, and dishonour the poor man. And this, speaking generally, is the way in which oligarchy is established.

Yes, he said; but what are the characteristics of this form of government, and what are the defects of which we were speaking?

First of all, I said, consider the nature of the qualification. Just think what would happen if pilots were to be chosen according to their property, and a poor man were refused permission to steer, even though he were a better pilot?

You mean that they would shipwreck?

Yes; and is not this true of the government of anything?

I should imagine so.

Except a state?—or would you include a state?

No, he said, the case of a city is the strongest of all, for the rule of a city is the greatest and most difficult of all.

This, then, will be the first great defect of oligarchy. And here is another defect which is quite as bad—the inevitable division: such a State is not one, but two States, the one of poor, the other of rich men; and they are living on the same spot and always conspiring against one another.

That, surely, is at least as bad.

Another discreditable feature is, that, for a like reason, they are incapable of carrying on any war. Either they arm the multitude, and then they are more afraid of them than of the enemy; or, if they do not call them out in the hour of battle, they are oligarchs indeed, few to fight as they are few to rule. And at the same time their fondness for money makes them unwilling to pay taxes.

How discreditable![1]

Plato then sketches the capitalist at his worst.

He takes to money-making and by mean and miserly savings and hard work gets a fortune together. Is not such an one likely to seat the greedy and covetous element of human nature on the throne and to suffer it to play the great king within him, girt with tiara and chain and scimitar? And when he has made reason and spirit[2] sit down on the ground obediently on either side of their sovereign, and taught them to know their place, he compels the one to think only of how lesser sums may be turned into larger ones, and will not allow the other to worship and admire anything but riches and rich men, or to be ambitious of anything so much as the acquisition of wealth and the means of acquiring it.[3]

4. *The Democratic State.*

Finally, the poor rise against the rich and plutocracy passes into democracy, which Plato considers worse than any form of government except despotism. The democracy which he criticizes is of course Athens, and his chief

[1] *Republic*, 550. [2] See p. 142 n.
[3] *Republic*, 553.

quarrel with it is that, whereas the ideal government is a state ruled by wisdom for the highest ends, the Athenian democracy has no ideal except freedom.

A portrait of democracy. (*The 'captain' is the electorate.*)

Imagine a fleet or a ship in which there is a captain who is taller and stronger than any of the crew, but he is a little deaf and his sight is weak, and his knowledge of navigation is not much better. The sailors are quarrelling with one another about the steering—every one is of opinion that he has a right to steer, though he has never learned the art of navigation and cannot tell who taught him or when he learned, and will further assert that it cannot be taught, and they are ready to make mincemeat of any one who says the contrary. They throng about the captain, begging and praying him to entrust the helm to them; and sometimes if they do not prevail, but others are preferred to them, they kill the others or throw them overboard, and having first chained up the noble captain's senses with drink or some narcotic, they mutiny and take possession of the ship and make free with the stores; thus, eating and drinking, they proceed on their voyage in such fashion as may be expected. Anyone who is their partisan and cleverly helps them in their plot for getting the ship out of the captain's hands into their own whether by force or persuasion, they compliment with the name of sailor, pilot, capable seaman, and they abuse those who take a different attitude and call them good-for-nothing; but that the true pilot must pay attention to the year and seasons and sky and stars and winds, and whatever else belongs to his art, if he intends to be really qualified for the command of a ship, and that he must and will be the steerer, whether other people like or not—the possibility of this union of authority with the steerer's art has never seriously entered into their thoughts or been made part of their calling. Now in vessels which are in a state of mutiny and by sailors who are mutineers, how will the true pilot be regarded? Will he not be called a prater, a star-gazer, a good-for-nothing?[1]

Some Weaknesses of Athenian Democracy

(*a*) *Its incompetence for good or evil.*

Government by the masses is feeble in every respect, and unable to do either any great good or any great evil, when compared with the others, because the offices are too minutely subdivided and too many hold them.[2]

(*b*) *Its tendency to excessive individualism, each man doing what is right in his own eyes.*

In the first place, a democracy is free; and the State is full of freedom and frankness—a man may say and do what he likes. And where freedom is, the individual is clearly able to order for himself his own life as he pleases, so that in this kind of State there will be the greatest variety of human character. Apparently it is the most beautiful of all constitutions—like a coloured dress embroidered with every sort of flower. And just as women and children think a variety of colours very lovely, so perhaps there are many men to whom this State,

[1] *Republic*, 488. [2] *Statesman*, 303.

embroidered with every kind of character, will appear to be the most beautiful of States. And it is the right kind of place in which to look for a constitution, because of the liberty which reigns there—they have a complete assortment of constitutions; and anyone who has a mind to found a State as we have been doing, might well go to a democracy as he would to a bazaar at which they sell them, and pick out the one that suits him; then, when he has made his choice, he may found his State. And there being no necessity for you to govern in this State, even if you have the capacity, or to be governed, unless you like, or to go to war when the rest go to war, or to be at peace when others are at peace, unless you are so disposed—there being no necessity also, because some law forbids you to hold office or sit on a jury, that you should not hold office or act as a juror, if you have a fancy—is not this a way of life which for the moment is supremely delightful? See too the forgiving spirit of democracy, and the 'don't care' about trifles, and the disregard which she shows of all the fine principles which we solemnly laid down at the foundation of the city—as when we said that, except in the case of some rarely gifted nature, there never will be a good man who has not from his childhood been used to play amid things of beauty and make of them a joy and a study—how grandly does she trample all these fine notions of ours under her feet, never giving a thought to the pursuits which make a statesman, and promoting to honour any one who professes to be the people's friend. These and other kindred characteristics are proper to democracy, which is a charming form of government, full of variety and disorder, and dispensing a sort of equality to equals and unequals alike.[1]

What Plato dislikes in Athenian democracy is its want of clear values and its failure to rule its life consistently by any high principle. The fact that his criticism may not be true of our politics should not blind us to the fact that it describes with painful accuracy the general life of our civilization. Witness that chaos of values, the cheap newspaper.

Familiar too in our world is the 'democratic man'—the man whose life is ruled by no principle. Plato regards him as the product of capitalism—the son of rich parents who reacts from their worship of wealth and at the same time discards their rigid puritan virtues.

So the young man passes out of his original nature, which was trained in the school of necessity, into the freedom and libertinism of useless and unnecessary pleasures. After this he lives on, spending his money and labour and time on unnecessary pleasures quite as much as on necessary ones; but if he is fortunate, and does not become too wild, when years have elapsed, and the heyday of passion is over—supposing that he then re-admits some of the exiled virtues, and does not wholly give himself up to their successors—in that case he balances his pleasures and lives in a sort of equilibrium, putting the government of himself into the hands of the one which comes first and wins the turn; and when he has had enough of that, then into the hands of another; he despises none of them but encourages them all equally. He

[1] *Republic*, 557 f.

will not admit into the fortress of his soul any true word of advice; if some one says to him that some pleasures are the satisfactions of good and noble desires, and others of evil desires, and that he ought to use and honour some and check and master the others—whenever this is repeated to him he shakes his head and says that they are all alike, and that one is as good as another. He lives from day to day indulging the appetite of the hour; and sometimes he is all for drink and jazz: then he becomes a water-drinker, and tries to get thin; then he takes a turn at gymnastics; sometimes idling and neglecting everything, then once more living the life of a philosopher; often he is busy with politics, and starts to his feet and says and does whatever comes into his head; or he conceives an admiration for the military life and off he goes in that direction, or for business, and turns to that. His life has neither law nor order; and this distracted existence he terms joy and bliss and freedom; and so he goes on. His life is motley and manifold and an epitome of many lives—he answers to the State which we described as fair and parti-coloured. Many a man and many a woman will take him for their pattern, and many a constitution and many an example of behaviour is contained in him. Let him then be set over against democracy; he may truly be called the democratic man.[1]

The following passage shows Plato's idea of freedom.

I would advise those who seek liberty and shun the yoke of servitude as evil, not to fall into the

[1] Ibid., 561.

plague of despotic rule, to which an insatiable passion of unseasonable freedom brought their fathers. In excess, servitude and liberty are each wholly bad; in due measure, each are wholly good. The due measure of servitude is to serve God, its excess is to serve man. Law is the god of the right-minded man; pleasure is the god of the fool.[1]

A further weakness in democracy is the irrationality of settling matters so intricate and important as political questions by the haphazard method of popular opinion.

The following passage criticizes the Athenian democracy with its popular vote and election by lot, its review of a statesman's conduct on the expiry of his office and the impeachment which frequently resulted. Finally, Plato comments on its dislike of any criticism of democratic institutions. Plato satirizes these traits by pointing out how absurd they would be if applied to medicine or seamanship. But if they would be ridiculous in dealing with health or transport, &c., are they not equally so in the far more complicated and difficult art of politics?

Let me have recourse to my favourite examples, the noble pilot and the doctor, 'who is worth many men', and observe in them an analogy to politics. Every man will reflect that we suffer terribly at the hands of both of them; the physician saves any whom he wishes to save, and any whom he wishes to maltreat he maltreats—operating and cauterising and at the same time requiring them to bring him fees, which are a sort of tribute, of which little or nothing is spent upon the sick man, and the greater part is con-

[1] *Letters*, viii. 354.

sumed by the doctor and his domestics. And the pilots of ships do the same sort of things times out of number; they intentionally play false and leave you ashore when the hour of sailing arrives; or they cause mishaps at sea and cast away their freight; and are guilty of other rogueries. Now suppose that we, bearing all this in mind, were to determine, after consideration, that neither of these arts shall any longer be allowed to exercise absolute control either over freemen or over slaves, but that we will summon an assembly either of all the people, or of the rich only, and that anybody who likes, whatever may be his calling, or even if he have no calling, may offer an opinion either about seamanship or about diseases—either as to the manner in which medicine or surgical instruments are to be applied to the patient, or again about ships and the nautical instruments which are required in navigation, and how to meet the dangers of winds and waves which are incidental to the voyage, how to behave when encountering pirates, and what is to be done with the old-fashioned galleys, if they have to fight with others of a similar build. Suppose too that the views of the crowd on these points, formed upon the advice of persons skilled or unskilled, are inscribed in the statute-book or adopted in unwritten form as national customs—that for all time to come vessels shall be navigated and remedies administered to the patient on these principles.

What a strange notion!

Suppose further, that the pilots and physicians are appointed annually, either out of the rich, or out of the whole people, and that they are elected by lot; and that after their election they navigate vessels and heal the sick according to the written rules.

Worse and worse.

But hear what follows:—When the year of office has expired, the pilot or physician has to come before a court of review, in which the judges are either selected from the wealthy classes or chosen by lot out of the whole people; and anybody who pleases may be their accuser, and may lay to their charge, that during the past year they have not navigated their vessels or healed their patients according to the letter of the law and the ancient customs of their ancestors; and if either of them is condemned, some of the judges must fix what he is to suffer or pay.

If a man is willing to take an office under such conditions, he deserves to suffer any penalty.

Further, if any one is detected making investigations into piloting and navigation, or into health and the true nature of medicine, or about the winds or temperature, contrary to the written rules, and conducting novel researches in these fields, we shall have to enact that he is not to be called a pilot or physician, but a cloudy prating sophist;—further, on the ground that he is a corrupter of the young, by persuading them to adopt an illegal attitude towards medicine or navigation, and to assume arbitrary power over their patients or ships, any one who is qualified by law may inform against him, and indict him before some court, and then if he is found to be persuading any, whether young or old, to act contrary to the written law, he is to be punished with the utmost rigour; for no one should presume to be wiser than the laws; every one, it will be said, knows the principles of health and piloting and navigation, for anybody may learn the written laws and the national usage in these subjects. If this was our attitude in the case of these sciences and in strategy or any branch of hunting, or in painting or other creative arts, or in carpentry, or any sort of handicraft, or in agriculture, or planting—I say, if our practice in all these fields was governed by written regulations what would be the result?

All our arts would be utterly ruined and irrevocably lost, because there was a law prohibiting any research into them. And human life, which is bad enough already, would then become completely unendurable.[1]

5. *The Despotic State.*

Excess of liberty leads to autocracy, and the licence of the democratic state ends in despotism. The following portrait of the despot might have been drawn from Hitler.

At first, in the early days of his power, the despot is full of smiles, and he salutes every one whom he meets;—he to be called a tyrant, who is making promises in public and in private! liberating debtors, and distributing land to the people and his followers, and wanting to be so kind and good to every one! But when he has disposed of foreign enemies by conquest or treaty, and there is nothing to fear from them, then he is always stirring up

[1] *Statesman*, 298 f.

some war or other, in order that the people may require a leader. And he has a further object, which is that they may be impoverished by payment of taxes, and so be compelled to devote themselves to their daily wants and therefore less likely to conspire against him. And if he suspects any one of having notions of freedom, and of resistance to his authority, he will have a good pretext for destroying them by placing them at the mercy of the enemy; and for all these reasons the tyrant must be always getting up a war.

Now he begins to grow unpopular, and some of those who joined in setting him up, and who are in power, speak their minds to him and to one another, and the more courageous of them criticize his actions to his face. The despot, if he means to rule, must get rid of them; he cannot stop while he has a friend or an enemy who is good for anything. And so he must look about him and see who is courageous, who is high-minded, who is wise, who is wealthy; happy man, he is the enemy of them all, and must plot against them whether he likes it or not, until he has purged the State—not with the sort of purge which the physicians make of the body; for they get rid of poisonous elements and leave the healthy part, but he does the reverse. If he is to rule, I suppose that he cannot help himself. What a blessed alternative, it is—to be compelled to live with associates mainly worthless who hate him, or else to lose his life! And the more odious his actions are to the citizens the more satellites and the greater devotion in them will he require. And how will the tyrant maintain that fine and numerous and various and ever-changing army of his? If there are sacred treasures[1] in the city, he will confiscate and spend them; and in so far as the fortunes of attainted persons may suffice, he will be able to diminish the taxes which he would otherwise have to impose upon the people. When these fail, he and his boon companions, male or female, will be maintained out of his father's estate.

You mean to say that the people, from whom he has derived his being, will maintain him and his companions?

Yes, he said; they cannot help themselves.

But what if the people fly into a passion, and declare that a grown-up son ought not to be supported by his father, but that the father should be supported by the son? The father did not bring him into being, or settle him in life, in order that when his son became a man he should himself be the servant of his own servants and should support him and his rabble of slaves and companions; but that his son should protect him, and that by his help he might be emancipated from the government of the rich and aristocratic, as they are termed. So the people orders the dictator and his friends to depart, just as any other father might drive out of the house a riotous son and his undesirable associates. And now they will discover to what a monster they have given birth and support and power, and find that they are weaker than the man whom they wish to expel.

Why, you do not mean to say that the tyrant will use violence? What! beat his father if he opposes him?

[1] Or, as we might say, 'church property'.

Yes, he will disarm and then beat him.

This is real tyranny, about which there can be no longer a mistake: as the saying is, the people who would escape the smoke which is the slavery of freemen, has fallen into the fire which is the tyranny of slaves. So liberty, getting out of all order and reason, passes into the harshest and bitterest form of slavery.[1]

Plato is more conscious of the defects of political institutions than of their merits: and his criticisms are better than his attempts at construction. His ideal is government by a perfectly wise ruler 'on scientific principles which follow the rules of wisdom and justice', but he sees that such people do not exist, and therefore that constitutional government is necessary. The following passage contains the conclusive objection both to anarchism and to autocracy whether of the Carlyle type or of less desirable kinds.

Mankind must have laws, and conform to them, or its life would be as bad as that of the most savage beast. And the reason of this is that no man's nature is able to know what is best for human society; or knowing, always able and willing to do what is best. In the first place, there is a difficulty in apprehending that a true social science is concerned, not with the individual but with the community (for public interest binds society together, while private interest only disrupts it); and that both the community and the individual gain when public, rather than private, interests are put first. In the second place, even if a person knows in the abstract that this is true, yet if he is

[1] *Republic*, 566 f.

possessed of absolute and irresponsible power, he will never remain firm in his principles or persist in regarding the public good as primary in the state, and individual interests as secondary. His human nature will be always driving him into self-aggrandisement and selfishness; he will avoid pain and pursue pleasure irrationally, and will make these considerations take precedence over what is just and good; and so, creating darkness in his soul, will at last fill with evils both it and the state. If, in God's providence, a man were born so gifted that he could naturally apprehend the truth, he would have no need of laws to govern him; for there is no law or regulation which is above knowledge, nor ought reason to be the subject or slave of any man; its right is to rule, if it really exists in its natural truth and liberty. But then there is no such reason anywhere, or very little of it; and so we must choose law and order, which are second best.[1]

Had Plato always remained of this opinion, he might have avoided the authoritarianism which is his great weakness as a political thinker. The following passage describes the powers of dealing with irreligion given to the Nocturnal Council (whose chief duty is to preserve the ideals of the state). It shows how closely Plato anticipated the Inquisition, and how, as with the Inquisition, admirable motives may lead to disastrous expedients.

If a man is guilty of any irreligion in word or deed, let any one who happens to be present give information to the magistrates, in aid of the law; and let the magistrates who first receive

[1] *Laws*, 875.

the information bring him before the appointed court according to the law; and if a magistrate, after receiving information, refuses to act, he shall be tried for irreligion at the instance of any one who is willing to vindicate the laws; and if any one be cast, the court shall estimate the punishment of each irreligious act; and let all such criminals be imprisoned. There shall be three prisons in the state: the first of them is to be the common prison in the neighbourhood of the market for the safe-keeping of ordinary criminals; another is to be in the neighbourhood of the Nocturnal Council, and is to be called the 'House of Reformation'; another, to be situated in some wild and desolate region in the centre of the country, shall be called by some name expressive of retribution. Now, irreligion is due to three causes, which have been already mentioned, and each of these causes leads to two sorts of irreligion (in all six), which are worth distinguishing, and should not all have the same punishment. A man who does not believe in the Gods, and yet is naturally upright, hates the wicked and dislikes and refuses to do wrong actions, and avoids bad men, and loves the good. But much worse are those who believe that there is no God in the world and at the same time have no self-control in the face of pleasure or pain, and also have good memories and quick wits; although both types are unbelievers, much less injury is done by the one than by the other. The one may talk loosely about the Gods and about sacrifices and oaths, and perhaps by laughing at other men he may make them like himself, if he goes unpunished. But the other who holds the same opinions and is called a clever man, is full of stratagem and deceit—men of this class deal in prophecy and jugglery of all kinds, and out of their ranks sometimes come despots and demagogues and hierophants of private mysteries and the Sophists, as they are termed, with their ingenious devices. There are many kinds of unbelievers, but two only for whom legislation is required; one the hypocritical sort, whose crime is deserving of death many times over, while the other needs only imprisonment and admonition. Similarly the notion that the Gods take no thought of men produces two other sorts of crimes, and the notion that they may be propitiated produces two more. Assuming these divisions, let those who have been made what they are only from want of intelligence, and not from malice or an evil nature, be placed by the judge in the House of Reformation, and ordered to suffer imprisonment during a period of not less than five years. In the meantime let them have no intercourse with the other citizens, except with members of the Nocturnal Council, and with them let them converse with a view to the improvement of their soul's health. And when the time of their imprisonment has expired, if any of them has recovered his senses let him be restored to sane company, but if not, and if he be condemned a second time, let him be punished with death. As to that class of monstrous natures who not only believe that there are no Gods, or that they are negligent, or to be propitiated, but in contempt of mankind conjure the souls of the living and say that they can conjure the dead and promise to charm the Gods with sacrifices and prayers, and will utterly overthrow individuals and whole houses and states for the sake of money—let him who is guilty of any of these crimes be condemned by the court to be immured according to law in the prison which is in the centre of the land, and let no freeman ever approach him, but let him receive the rations of food appointed by the guardians of the law from the hands of the public slaves; and when he is dead let him be cast beyond the borders unburied, and if any freeman assist in burying him, let him pay the penalty of irreligion to any one who is willing to bring a suit against him. But if he leaves behind him children who are fit to be citizens, let the guardians of orphans take care of them, just as they would of any other orphans, from the day on which their father is convicted.[1]

The Economics of the Ideal State

Plato holds as strongly as any Christian moralist that money is a chief source of evil.

The intention, as we affirm, of a reasonable statesman, is not what is popularly held to be the object of a good legislator, namely, that the state for the true interests of which he is advising should be as great and as rich as possible, and should possess gold and silver, and have the greatest empire by sea and land;—this they imagine to be the real object of legislation, at the same time adding, inconsistently, that the true legislator desires to have the city the best and happiest possible. The citizen must indeed be happy and good, and

[1] *Laws*, 907 f.

the legislator will seek to make him so; but very rich and very good at the same time he cannot be, not, at least, in the sense in which most men speak of riches. For they mean by 'the rich' the small minority whose property is worth a great deal of money—just what a rogue might equally well own. But if so, I can never assent to the doctrine that the rich man will be happy—he must be good as well as rich. And good in a high degree, and rich in a high degree at the same time, he cannot be. Some one will ask, why not? And we shall answer,—Because acquisitions which come from sources which are just and unjust indifferently, are more than double those which come from just sources only; and the sums which are expended neither honourably nor disgracefully, are only half as great as those which are expended honourably and on honourable purposes. Thus, if the one acquires double and spends half, the other who is in the opposite case and is a good man cannot possibly be wealthier than he. The first—I am speaking of the saver and not of the spender—is not always bad; he may indeed in some cases be utterly bad, but, as I was saying, a good man he never is. For he who receives money unjustly as well as justly, and spends neither justly nor unjustly, will be a rich man if he be also thrifty. On the other hand, the utterly bad is in general profligate, and therefore very poor; while he who spends on noble objects and acquires wealth by just means only, can hardly be remarkable for riches, any more than he can be very poor. Our statement, then, is true, that the very rich are not good, and, if they are not good, they are not happy. But the intention of our laws was, that the citizens should be as happy as may be, and as united as possible. And there can be no friendly relations in a state where lawsuits and injustice abound—only where they are few and insignificant. So we say that gold and silver ought not to be allowed in the state, nor much of the money-making which depends on usury or mechanical trades; but only the produce and profits of agriculture, and only so much of this as will not compel us in pursuing it to neglect that for the sake of which riches exist,—I mean, soul and body, which without physical and other education, will never be worth anything; and so, as we have said many times, the care of riches should have the last place in our thoughts. For there are three things in which every man is interested; the interest about money, when rightly regarded, is the third and lowest of them: midway comes the interest of the body; and, first of all, that of the soul; and the state which we are describing will have been rightly constituted if it ordains honours on this principle. But if, in any of the laws which have been ordained, health has been preferred to temperance, or wealth to health and temperate habits, that law must clearly be wrong. So the legislator ought often to impress upon himself the question—'What do I want?' and 'Do I attain my aim, or do I miss the mark?'[1]

The community which has neither poverty nor wealth will always have the noblest characters; in it there is no pride or injustice, nor, again, is there competitiveness or jealousy.[2]

[1] *Laws*, 247. [2] Ibid., 679.

In a state which wishes to avoid the greatest of all curses—not faction, but rather disruption—there should exist among the citizens neither extreme poverty, nor, again, excess of wealth, for both are productive of both these evils.[1]

Actually Plato will allow the wealthiest man in his state to be four times as rich as the poorest.

The greatest cause of crime is lust, which gets the mastery of a soul maddened by desire; and this is most commonly found to exist where that passion reigns which is strongest and most prevalent among the mass of mankind: I mean where the power of wealth breeds endless desires of unlimited and insatiable acquisition, originating in natural disposition, and a miserable want of education. Of this want of education, the false praise of wealth which is bruited about both among Hellenes and barbarians is the cause; they rank as the first of good things that which in reality is only third. And in this way they wrong both posterity and themselves, for there can be nothing nobler and better for any state than that the truth about wealth should be proclaimed there—the truth that riches are for the service of the body, and that the body is for the service of the soul. They are good, and wealth is intended by nature to serve them, and it is therefore inferior to them both, and takes the third place. This doctrine teaches us that he who would be happy ought not to seek wealth, or rather he should seek wealth justly won and temperately used.[2]

[1] Ibid., 744.

[2] Ibid., 870.

The Problem of Commerce

Retail trade in a city is not by nature intended to do any harm, but quite the contrary; for is not he a benefactor who reduces the inequalities and incommensurabilities of goods to equality and common measure? And this is what the power of money effects, and this is the task assigned to the merchant. The wage-earner and the innkeeper, and many other occupations, some of them more and others less respectable—all alike have this object;—they seek to satisfy our needs and equalize our possessions. Let us then try to see what has brought retail trade into disrepute, and why it is regarded as ignoble and discreditable, in order that we may at least yet partially cure the evil by legislation. This is no easy matter. For small, my dear Cleinias—they must be rarely gifted by nature and supremely well-educated—is the class of men who can steadily set their faces towards moderation when they are assailed by some need or desire, and who, when they have a chance of making large sums of money, prefer a moderate competence to great wealth. The mass of mankind is the exact opposite of this; what they want they want immoderately, and they are insatiable in their wish to make money, when moderate profits are in their reach. That is why the whole business of retail trade, commerce and innkeeping is abused and discredited. Suppose—an absurd supposition, but I will make it—suppose that some one compelled the best men everywhere to engage for a time in retail trade or in similar work, or that a preordained law of nature forced women to take to some such way of life. We should then recognize how friendly and acceptable all these occupations are; and if they were managed on incorruptible principles, we should honour them as we honour a mother or a nurse. At present, for trade purposes men plant houses in lonely spots at the centre of long stretches of road.[1] They entertain distressed travellers with welcome shelter. They afford a cool refuge in the heats of summer and a calm and sunny retreat to wayfarers buffeted by wild and violent storms. Then, after receiving them as friends, instead of providing friendly entertainment to match their reception, they treat them like defeated captive enemies, and extort huge, unjust and abominable ransoms. It is these and similar practices that have brought into discredit occupations that in fact are the relief of human needs. The statesman ought always to be devising a remedy for evils of this nature. There is an ancient saying, which is also a true one—'To fight against two opponents is a difficult thing'; we see this in disease and in many other instances. And in this case also the war is against two enemies—wealth and poverty; one of which corrupts the soul of man with luxury, while the other drives him through suffering into utter shamelessness. What remedy can the wise state find against this disease? In the first place, they must have as few retail traders as possible; and in the second place, they must assign the occupation to that class of men whose corruption will be the least injury to the state; and in the third place, they must devise some way whereby

[1] A description of a Greek inn.

the followers of these occupations themselves will not readily fall into habits of unbridled shamelessness and meanness.[1]

The Only Sound Basis of Economic Change.

Another piece of good fortune is that we have escaped confiscation of estates and cancellation of debts; for these are always a source of dangerous contention, and a city which is driven by necessity to legislate upon such matters can neither allow the old ways to continue, nor yet venture to alter them. All that can be done is to hope and to aim at slight and cautious change over a long period. If among those in favour of change there are persons with large estates and a number of creditors, they should be willing, in a liberal spirit, to share with those who are in want, sometimes remitting and sometimes giving, holding fast the path of moderation, and regarding poverty as the increase of a man's desires and not the diminution of his property. For this is the great foundation of social security to a state, and upon this lasting basis may be erected afterwards whatever political order is suitable under the circumstances; but if the change be based upon an unsound principle, the future administration of the country will be full of difficulties. Let me now definitely assert that no other way of escape, whether narrow or broad, can be devised but freedom from avarice and a sense of justice—upon this rock our city shall be built.[2]

The Position of Women

Never does Plato show his clearsightedness and power of following reason, than when, living in a state

[1] *Laws*, 918 f. [2] Ibid., 736.

where women had no education or share in public life, he anticipates the view of their place in society which the world did not reach for 2,000 years more.

Are dogs divided into hes and shes, or do they both share equally in hunting and in keeping watch and in the other duties of dogs? or do we entrust to the males the entire and exclusive care of the flocks, while we leave the females at home, under the idea that the bearing and suckling their puppies is labour enough for them?

No, he said, they share alike; the only difference between them is that the males are stronger and the females weaker.

But can you use different animals for the same purpose, unless they are bred and fed in the same way?

You cannot.

Then, if women are to have the same duties as men, they must have the same up-bringing and education, and as the education which was assigned to the men was music and gymnastic, so women must be taught music and gymnastic and also the art of war, which they must practise like the men.[1]

Plato then puts the Objection to his View

Our opponents will say: 'Socrates and Glaucon, no adversary need convict you, for you yourselves, at the first foundation of the State, admitted the principle that everybody was to do the one work suited to his own nature.' And certainly, if I am not mistaken, such an admission was made by us. 'And do not the natures of men and women differ

[1] *Republic*, 451. For the meaning of 'music' see p. 109 n.

very much indeed?' And we shall reply: Of course they do. Then we shall be asked, 'Whether the tasks assigned to men and to women should not be different, and such as are suitable to their different natures?' Certainly they should. 'But if so, have you not fallen into a serious inconsistency in saying that men and women, whose natures are so entirely different, ought to have the same activities?'—What defence will you make for us, my good Sir, against any one who offers these objections?[1]

To this Plato replies

Among the various occupations in the life of the state there is none which belongs to woman as woman or to man as man: the gifts of nature are alike distributed in both; all the pursuits of men are open to women also, but in all of them a woman is inferior to a man. Then are we to impose all our enactments on men and none of them on women?

That will never do.

One woman has a gift of healing, another not; one is a musician, and another has no music in her nature. One woman has a turn for gymnastic and military exercises, and another is unwarlike and hates gymnastics. One woman is a philosopher,[2] and another detests philosophy; one has

[1] *Republic*, 453.

[2] Plato holds that there are three human temperaments; the 'philosophic', or intellectual, which produces thinkers, men of science, artists, and statesmen; the 'spirited', or pugnacious, adventurous, fearless temper, that makes good soldiers; the 'appetitive', which pursues money or pleasure. In his commonwealth the 'philosophic' will rule the state, the 'spirited' will defend it; the rest are not fit for either function.

the active temperament, and another has it not. Then one woman will have the temper of a ruler, and another not. Was not the selection of the male rulers determined by differences of this sort? Men and women alike possess the qualities which make rulers; they differ only in their comparative strength or weakness. And those women who have such qualities are to be selected as the companions and colleagues of men who have similar qualities and whom they resemble in capacity and in character. The same natures ought to have the same pursuits, and so there is nothing unnatural in assigning music and gymnastic to the wives of the ruling class, and the law which we enacted was agreeable to nature, and therefore not an impossibility or mere aspiration; and the contrary practice, which prevails at present, is in reality a violation of nature.

So let the wives of our rulers strip, for their virtue will be their dress, and let them share in the toils of war and the defence of their country; only in the distribution of labours the lighter are to be assigned to the women, who are the weaker natures, but in other respects their duties are to be the same.[1]

Nothing can be more absurd than the practice which prevails in our own country, of men and women not following the same pursuits with all their strength and with one mind, for thus the state, instead of being a whole, is reduced to a half, but has the same taxes to pay and the same toils

[1] Ibid., 455 f.

to undergo; and what can be a greater mistake for any legislator to make than this?[1]

War

War, whether external or civil, is something we must pray to escape: peace with one another, and good will, are best. The victory of the state over itself may be a necessity but is not a really good thing; a man might as well say that the body was in the best state when sick and purged by medicine, forgetting that there is also a state of the body which needs no purge. And similarly no one can be a true statesman, whether he aims at the happiness of the individual or state, who looks only, or first of all, to external warfare; nor will he ever be a sound legislator who orders peace for the sake of war, and not war for the sake of peace.[2]

[1] *Laws*, 805.

[2] Ibid., 628.

CHAPTER V

EDUCATION

Plato is the first man to have seen the importance of education and to make it central in his political philosophy. The following extracts show how much of modern educational theory he anticipated.

The Need of Education

If a man neglects education he walks lame to the end of his life, and returns imperfect and good for nothing to the world below.[1]

True Education

Plato's point here is that education is not the implanting of knowledge; it is, in its deepest sense, the conversion of the whole mind from the shows and shadows of the changing world to the eternal realities.

Certain professors of education must be wrong when they say that they can put a knowledge into the soul which was not there before, like sight into blind eyes. Whereas, our argument shows that the power and faculty of learning exists in the soul already; and that just as the eye was unable to turn from darkness to light without the whole body turning with it, so the faculty of knowledge can only by the movement of the whole soul be turned from the world of change to that of reality, and learn by degrees to endure the sight of reality, and of what is brightest and best in it, or in other words, of the Idea of the

[1] *Timaeus*, 44.

Good.[1] And must there not be some art which will effect conversion in the easiest and quickest manner; not implanting the faculty of sight, for that exists already, but has been turned in the wrong direction, and is looking away from the truth? And while the other so-called virtues of the soul seem to be akin to bodily qualities, for even when they are not originally innate they can be implanted later by habit and exercise, the virtue of wisdom more than anything else contains a divine element which always remains, and by this conversion is rendered useful and profitable; otherwise it remains hurtful and useless. Did you never observe the narrow intelligence flashing from the keen eye of a clever rogue—how eager he is, how clearly his paltry soul sees the way to his end; he is the reverse of blind, but his keen eye-sight is forced into the service of evil, and he is mischievous in proportion to his cleverness? But what if there had been a circumcision of such natures in their youth; and they had been cut off from those sensual pleasures, such as eating and drinking, which, like leaden weights, were attached to them at their birth, and which drag them down and turn the vision of their souls upon the things that are below—if, I say, they had been released from these impediments and turned in the opposite direction, the very same faculty in them would have seen the truth as keenly as they see what their eyes are turned to now.[2]

The Ideal of Liberal Education

We must not be indefinite about the meaning of education. At present, when we are criticizing

[1] See p. 47. [2] *Republic*, 518 f.

or praising a man's upbringing, we call one person educated and another uneducated, although the latter may be sometimes very well educated for the calling of a retail trader, or of a captain of a ship, and the like. But we are not speaking of education in this narrower sense, but of that other education in virtue from youth upwards, which makes a man passionately desire to be the perfect citizen, and teaches him how rightly to rule and how to obey. This is the only education which, upon our view, deserves the name; that other sort of training, which aims at the acquisition of wealth or bodily strength, or mere cleverness apart from intelligence and justice, is mean and illiberal, and is not worthy to be called education at all. But let us not quarrel with one another about a word, provided that the proposition which has just been granted hold good: I mean, that those who are rightly educated generally become good men. And we must never disparage education, which is the first and fairest thing that the best of men can ever have; it may take a wrong direction, but it can be reformed. And this work of reformation is the great business of every man while he lives.[1]

Early Training

Pleasure and pain I maintain to be the first perceptions of children, and I say that they are the forms under which virtue and vice first come into their lives. As to wisdom and true beliefs, happy is the man who acquires them, even in old age; and we may say that he who possesses them, and the blessings which they bring, is a perfect

[1] *Laws*, 643 f.

man. Now I mean by education that training which is given by suitable habits to the first instincts of virtue in children;—when the right pleasures and pains, likes and dislikes, are implanted in souls not yet capable of understanding the nature of them, and who find them, after they have attained reason, to be in harmony with her. This harmony of the soul, taken as a whole, is virtue; but the particular training in respect of pleasure and pain, which leads you always to hate what you ought to hate, and love what you ought to love from the beginning of life to the end, may be separated off; and, in my view, will be rightly called education.[1]

Cle. How must the state educate those who do not as yet understand language, and are therefore incapable of appreciating any sort of instruction?

Ath. I will tell you how:—Every creature that is born has a habit of expressing itself by making a noise—human babies above all; and it is their way to cry as well as to scream. Do not nurses, when they wish to know what a baby wants, judge by these signs?—when anything is brought to it and it is silent, then it is supposed to be pleased, but when it weeps and cries out, then it is displeased. For tears and cries are the ominous signs by which children show what they love and hate. This goes on for not less than three years, and that is a considerable portion of life to be passed ill or well. Now don't you think that difficult and ungracious natures are more prone

[1] *Laws*, 653.

to complaints and self-pity than a good man ought to be?

Cle. Certainly.

Ath. Well, but if during these three years every possible care were taken that our nursling should have as little of sorrow and fear, and in general of pain as was possible, might we not expect in early childhood to make his soul more gentle and cheerful?

Cle. Certainly—especially if we could procure him a variety of pleasures.

Ath. There I can no longer agree, Cleinias: you amaze me. To bring him up in such a way would be his utter ruin; for the beginning is always the most critical part of education. The point about which you and I differ is of great importance. For I maintain that the true life should neither seek for pleasures, nor, on the other hand, entirely avoid pains, but should embrace an intermediate state, which I just now spoke of as gracious—a state which a prophetic saying leads us to ascribe to God. Now, I say that those of us who aspire to the divine ought to aim at this intermediate condition—we should not rush headlong into pleasure, as though we could be free from pain; nor should we allow any one, young or old, male or female, to be thus given any more than ourselves, and least of all the newly-born infant, for in infancy more than at any other time the character is implanted through habit.[1]

Education is the drawing and directing of youth towards that right reason, which the law affirms,

[1] Ibid., 791 f.

and which the experience of the eldest and best has agreed, to be truly right. Our aim is that the soul of the child may not be habituated to feel joy and sorrow in a manner at variance with the law, and those who obey the law, but may rather follow the law and rejoice and sorrow at the same things as their elders. That is the object of our songs. They are spells for souls, and are designed to implant that harmony of which we speak. And, because the mind of the child is incapable of enduring serious training, they are called play and song, and are performed in play. On the same principle those in charge of persons who are ill or in poor physical condition administer to their patients the nourishment that is good for them in the form of pleasant food and drink, while they disguise unsuitable food in an unattractive form, so that they may learn, as they ought, to like the one, and to dislike the other. So the true legislator will persuade, and, if he cannot persuade, will compel the poet rightly to express by fair and noble words, in his rhythms the attitude, and in his melodies the music, of temperate and brave and in every way good men.[1]

This discipline of pleasure and pain which, when rightly ordered, is a principle of education, has been often relaxed and corrupted in human life. And the Gods, pitying the toils which our race is born to undergo, have appointed holy festivals, in which men alternate rest with labour. On this point I should like to know whether a common saying is in our opinion true to nature or not.

[1] *Laws*, 659 f.

Men say that the young of all creatures cannot keep their bodies or their tongues quiet; they are always wanting to move and cry out; some leaping and skipping, and overflowing with playfulness and pleasure, others uttering all sorts of cries. But, whereas animals have no perception of order or disorder in their movements, that is, of rhythm or harmony, as they are called, to us, the Gods, who, as we say, have been appointed to be our companions in the dance, have given the pleasurable sense of harmony and rhythm; and so they stir us into life, and we follow them, joining hands together in dance and song. Education is first given through Apollo and the Muses, and a properly educated man will be able to sing and dance well.[1]

Knowledge which is acquired under compulsion obtains no hold on the mind. So do not use compulsion, but let early education be a sort of amusement.[2]

These passages and the one which follows show how completely Plato had anticipated modern views on unconscious education.

Are the poets alone to be required by us to express the likeness of the good in their works, on pain, if they do anything else, of expulsion from our State? Or is the same control to be extended to other artists, and are they also to be prohibited from exhibiting the opposite forms of vice and intemperance and meanness and indecency in

[1] Ibid., 653 f. [2] *Republic*, 536.

sculpture and building and the other creative arts; and is he who cannot conform to this rule of ours to be prevented from practising his art in our State, lest the taste of our citizens be corrupted by him? We would not have our rulers grow up amid images of moral deformity, as in some noxious pasture, and there browse and feed upon many a poisonous herb and flower day by day, little by little, until they silently gather a festering mass of corruption in their own soul. Let our artists rather be those who are gifted to discern the true nature of beauty and grace; then will our youth dwell in a land of health, amid fair sights and sounds, and receive the good in everything; and beauty, the effluence of fair works, shall flow into the eye and ear, like a health-giving breeze from a purer region, and insensibly draw the soul from earliest years into likeness and sympathy with the beauty of reason.[1]

The Two Sides of Education

When a man allows music[2] to play upon him and to pour into his soul through the funnel of his ears those sweet and soft and melancholy airs of which we were just now speaking, and his whole life is passed in warbling and the delights of song; in the first stage of the process the spirited element[3] which is in him is tempered like iron, and made useful, instead of brittle and useless. But, if he carries on the softening and soothing process, a stage of softening and wasting sets in, which dissolves his spirit and cuts out the sinews of his soul; and he becomes a feeble fighter. If the element of

[1] *Republic*, 401. [2] See p. 109 n. [3] See p. 142 n.

spirit is naturally weak in him the change takes place quickly, but if he have a good deal, then the power of music weakening the spirit renders him excitable;—on the least provocation he flames up at once, but the fire dies quickly down; instead of having spirit he grows irritable and passionate and difficult. And so in gymnastics, if a man takes violent exercise and dines well, and has no contact with music and philosophy, at first the high condition of his body fills him with pride and spirit, and he becomes twice the man that he was. And what happens? if he do nothing else, and holds no converse with the Muses, even such intelligence as he has, having no taste of any sort of learning or enquiry or thought or culture, grows feeble and dull and blind, his mind is never aroused or fed, and his senses are unpurged of their mists. And he ends by becoming a hater of philosophy, uncivilized, never using the weapon of persuasion, —he is like a wild beast, all violence and fierceness, and knows no other way of dealing; and he lives an ignorant and clumsy life, devoid of harmony and grace. And as there are two principles of human nature, one the spirited and the other the philosophical, some God, as I should say, has given mankind two arts answering to them (and only secondarily to the soul and body), in order that these two principles (like the strings of an instrument) may be relaxed or drawn tighter until they are duly harmonized. And the man who combines music with gymnastic in the fairest proportions, and best attempers them to the soul, may be rightly called the true musician and harmonist in a far higher sense than the tuner of the strings;

and such a presiding genius will be always required in our State if the government is to last.[1]

Some Subjects of Education

(*a*) *Arithmetic.*

Above all, Arithmetic arouses sleepy and dull natures, and makes them quick to learn, retentive, shrewd, and has an amazing way of causing them to progress quite beyond their natural powers.[2]

Have you observed, that those who have a natural talent for calculation are generally quick at every other kind of knowledge; and even dull pupils, if they have had an arithmetical training, although they may derive no other advantage from it, always become much quicker than they would otherwise have been? You will not easily find a more difficult study, and not many as difficult, and, for all these reasons, arithmetic is a kind of knowledge in which the best natures should be trained.[3]

(*b*) Geometry also concerns us: part of it relates to war; for in pitching a camp, or taking up a position, or closing or extending the lines of an army, or any other military manœuvre, whether in actual battle or on a march, it will make all the difference whether a general is or is not a geometrician. But for that purpose a very little of either geometry or calculation will be enough; we are concerned rather with the greater and more advanced part of geometry—whether that tends in any degree to make more easy the vision of the

[1] *Republic*, 411 f.

[2] *Laws*, 750. Plato is speaking, not of Arithmetic in our sense, but of the Theory of Number.

[3] *Republic*, 526.

Idea of Good; and thither, as I was saying, all things tend which compel the soul to turn her gaze towards that place, where is the full perfection of reality, which she ought, by all means, to behold. Anybody who has the least acquaintance with geometry will not deny that such a conception of the science is in flat contradiction to the ordinary language of geometricians. They have in view practice only, and are always speaking, in a narrow and ridiculous manner, of squaring and extending and applying and the like—they confuse the necessities of geometry with those of daily life; whereas knowledge is the real object of the whole science. The knowledge at which geometry aims is knowledge of the eternal, and not of anything perishing and transient. It will draw the soul towards truth, and create the spirit of philosophy.[1]

(*c*) *Philosophy.*

At present the students of philosophy are quite young; beginning when they are hardly past childhood, they pursue it in the interval before they engage in moneymaking and managing their estates; and even those of them who are reputed to have most of the philosophic spirit, when they come within sight of the most advanced and difficult parts of the subject, abandon the study. In after life when invited by some one else, they may, perhaps, go and hear a lecture, and about this they make much ado, for philosophy is not considered by them to be their proper business: at last, when

[1] Ibid. Plato's idea is that an abstract subject like geometry turns the mind from the particular to the universal, from phenomena to the laws behind them.

they grow old, in most cases they are extinguished more completely than Heraclitus' sun, inasmuch as they never light up again.[1]

But what ought to be their course?

Just the opposite. In childhood and youth their study and the philosophy they learn, should be suited to their tender years: during this period while they are growing up towards manhood, the chief and special care should be given to their bodies that they may have them to use in the service of philosophy; as life advances and the intellect begins to mature, let them increase the gymnastics of the soul.[2]

Another reason why Plato wishes to postpone the study of philosophy appears in the following passage which describes a phenomenon familiar to every university teacher and sometimes seen in the teachers themselves.

There is a danger lest they should taste the dear delight of dialectic too early; for youngsters, as you may have observed, when they first get the taste in their mouths, argue for amusement, and are always contradicting and refuting others in imitation of those who refute them; like puppy-dogs, they rejoice in pulling and tearing at all who come near them. And when they have won many victories and received many defeats, they violently and speedily get into a way of not believing anything which they believed before, and hence, not only they, but philosophy and all that relates to it is apt to have a bad name with the rest of the world. But when a man begins to get older, he

[1] Heraclitus, an early Greek thinker, thought that the sun was extinguished at sunset.

[2] *Republic*, 498.

will no longer be guilty of such insanity; he will imitate the thinker who is seeking for truth, and not the debater, who is contradicting for the sake of amusement.[1]

A Picture of Greek Education

Education commences in the first years of childhood, and lasts to the very end of life. Mother and nurse and father and tutor are vying with one another about the improvement of the child as soon as ever he is able to understand what is being said to him: he cannot say or do anything without their setting forth to him that this is just and that is unjust; this is honourable, that is dishonourable; this is holy, that is unholy; do this and abstain from that. And if he obeys, well and good; if not, he is straightened by threats and blows, like a piece of bent or warped wood. At a later stage they send him to teachers, and tell them to see to his manners even more than to his reading and music; and the teachers do as they are desired. And when the boy has learned his letters and is beginning to understand what is written, as before he understood only what was spoken, they put into his hands the works of great poets, which he reads sitting on a bench at school; in these are contained many admonitions, and many tales, and praises, and encomia of ancient famous men, which he is required to learn by heart, in order that he may imitate or emulate them and desire to become like them. Then, again, the teachers of the lyre take similar care that their young dis-

[1] *Republic*, 539.

ciple is temperate and gets into no mischief; and when they have taught him the use of the lyre, they introduce him to the poems of other excellent poets, who are the lyric poets; and these they set to music, and make their harmonies and rhythms quite familiar to the children's souls, in order that they may learn to be more gentle, and harmonious, and rhythmical, and so more fitted for speech and action; for the life of man in every part has need of harmony and rhythm. Then they send them to the master of gymnastic, in order that their bodies may better minister to the virtuous mind, and that they may not be compelled through bodily weakness to play the coward in war or on any other occasion. This is what is done by those who have the means, and those who have the means are the rich; their children begin to go to school soonest and leave off latest. When they have done with masters, the state again compels them to learn the laws, and live after the pattern which these furnish, and not after their own fancies; and just as in learning to write, the writing-master first draws lines for the use of the young beginner, and gives him the tablet and makes him follow the lines, so the city draws the laws, which were the invention of good lawgivers living in the olden time; these are given to the young man, in order to guide him in his conduct whether he is commanding or obeying; and he who transgresses them is to be corrected, or, in other words, called to account, which is a term used not only in your country, but also in many others, seeing that justice calls men to account.[1]

[1] *Protagoras*, 325 f. Protagoras is the speaker.

Education in the Platonic State

(*a*) *The Minister of Education.*

There remains the minister of the education of youth, male and female; he too will rule according to law; one such minister will be sufficient, and he must be fifty years old, and have children lawfully begotten, both boys and girls by preference, at any rate, one or the other. He who is elected, and he who is the elector, should consider that of all the great offices of state this is the greatest; for the first shoot of any plant, if it makes a good start towards the attainment of its natural excellence, has the greatest effect on its maturity; and this is not only true of plants, but of animals wild and tame, and also of men. Man, as we say, is a tame or civilized animal; nevertheless, he requires proper instruction and a fortunate nature, and then of all animals he becomes the most divine and most civilized; but if he is insufficiently or ill educated he is the most savage of earthly creatures. So the legislator ought not to allow the education of children to become a secondary or casual matter. In the first place, he should begin by taking care that the choice falls on the citizen who is in every way most suitable for the post.[1] The legislator shall do his utmost to appoint him minister and superintendent of education. To this end all the magistrates shall go to the temple of Apollo, and elect by ballot him of the guardians of the law whom they severally think will be the best superintendent of education. And he who has the

[1] A Platonic suggestion which is hardly ever followed in England.

greatest number of votes, after he has undergone a scrutiny at the hands of all the magistrates who have been his electors, with the exception of the guardians of the law,—shall hold office for five years; and in the sixth year let another be chosen in like manner to fill his office.[1]

(*b*) *The pupils.*

Neither sheep nor any other animals can live without a shepherd, nor can children be left without tutors, or slaves without masters. And of all animals the boy is the most unmanageable, inasmuch as he has the fountain of reason in him not yet regulated; he is the most insidious, sharp-witted, and insubordinate of animals. So he must be bound with many bridles; in the first place, when he gets away from mothers and nurses, he must be under the management of tutors on account of his childishness and foolishness; then, again, being a freeman, he must be controlled by teachers.[2]

(*c*) *The Schools. Plato has partly anticipated the English public school.*

Next follow the buildings for schools open to all; these are to be in three places in the midst of the city; and outside the city and in the surrounding country, also in three places, there shall be schools for horse exercise, and large grounds arranged with a view to archery and the throwing of missiles, at which young men may learn and practise. In these several schools let there be quarters for teachers, who shall be brought from

[1] *Laws*, 765 f.
[2] Ibid. 808.

foreign parts by pay, and let them teach those who attend the schools the art of war and the art of music,[1] and the children shall come not only if their parents please, but if they do not please; there shall be compulsory education, as the saying is, of all and sundry, as far as this is possible; and the pupils shall be regarded as belonging to the state rather than to their parents.[2]

[1] See p. 109 n.
[2] *Laws*, 804.

CHAPTER VI

MORAL IDEALS

Is might or right to prevail in politics? That is the chief political question of to-day. It is the issue between us and Germany. But in different forms it is a question for each individual in his own life. Why be good rather than bad? Why recognize any standard except self-interest?

It was also a burning question in Plato's day, when many thinkers held that 'justice' is artificial, a mere human creation, and that by the law of nature the strong rule and take what they can. In politics, said Thucydides, 'the strong do what they can and the weak suffer what they must.'

There is no better discussion of this problem than Plato's. He puts bluntly and powerfully the philosophy of Hitler and Mussolini. The speaker is a contemporary Athenian politician (Callicles).

The makers of laws are the majority, who are weak; and they make laws and distribute praise and censure with a view to themselves and to their own interests; and they terrify the stronger sort of men, and those who could oppress them, in order to escape oppression; and they say, that oppression is shameful and unjust; meaning, by the word injustice, the desire of a man to get the better of his neighbours; for, inferiors as they are, they are satisfied, I suppose, if they can have equality. And so the endeavour to get the better of the masses is conventionally said to be shameful and unjust, and is called injustice, whereas nature herself indicates that it is just for the better and the more powerful to dominate worse and weaker individuals; and in many ways she shows, among men as well as among animals, and indeed among whole cities and races, that justice consists in the superior ruling over and getting the better of the inferior. For on what principle of justice did Xerxes invade Greece, or his father the Scythians? (not to speak of numberless other examples). These are the men who act according to nature; yes, by Heaven, and according to the law of nature: not, perhaps, according to that artificial law, which we invent and impose upon our fellows, of whom we take the best and strongest from their youth upwards, and tame them like young lions,—charming them with the sound of the voice, and saying to them, that they must be content with equality, and that equality is honourable and just. But if there were a man who had sufficient force, he would shake off and break through, and escape from all this; he would trample under foot all our formulas and spells and charms, and all our laws which are against nature: the slave would rise in rebellion and be lord over us, and the light of natural justice would shine forth.[1]

A man who wishes really to live should give his passions full latitude of development and not restrain them; but when they have grown to their greatest he should have courage and intelligence to minister to them and to satisfy all his desires. This is what Nature means by justice and nobility.

[1] *Gorgias*, 483.

To this however the masses cannot attain; and they blame the strong man because they are ashamed of their own weakness; they want to conceal it, and so they say that immorality is shameful. As I have remarked already, they enslave the nobler natures, and because they are unable to satisfy their pleasures, they praise temperance and justice out of their own cowardice. For if a man had been originally the son of a king, or had a nature capable of acquiring an empire or a despotism or sovereign power, what could be more truly shameful or evil than temperance—to a man like him, I say, who might freely be enjoying every good, and has no one to stand in his way, and yet has allowed custom and reason and the opinion of other men to be lords over him?—must not he be wretched if the 'nobility' of justice and temperance hinders him from favouring his friends over his enemies, even though he is the ruler of his state? You, Socrates, profess to be a votary of the truth, and the truth is this:—that luxury and intemperance and licence, if they are provided with means, are virtue and happiness—all the rest is a mere bauble, a convention which Nature disowns, foolish talk of men, worth nothing.[1]

The Same View put more subtly and plausibly

That those who are just are so involuntarily and because they have not the power to be unjust will best appear if we imagine something of this kind. Let us give both the just and the unjust power to do what they will, and then watch and see where desire will lead them; then we shall dis-

[1] *Gorgias*, 492.

cover in the very act the just and unjust man proceeding along the same road, following their interest, which all natures regard as their good, and are only diverted into the path of justice by the force of law. The liberty which we are supposing may be most completely given to them in the form of such a power as is said to have been possessed by Gyges, the ancestor of Croesus the Lydian. According to the tradition, Gyges was a shepherd in the service of the king of Lydia; there was a great storm, and an earthquake made an opening in the earth at the place where he was feeding his flock. Amazed at the sight, he descended into the opening, where, among other marvels, he saw a hollow brazen horse, with doors in it. Stooping and looking in he saw a dead body of stature, as appeared to him, more than human, and having nothing on but a gold ring; this he took from the finger of the dead man and reascended. Now the shepherds met together, according to custom, that they might send their monthly report about the flocks to the king; into their assembly he came with the ring on his finger, and as he was sitting among them he chanced to turn the collet of the ring inside his hand, when instantly he became invisible to the rest of the company and they began to speak of him as if he were no longer present. He was astonished at this, and again touching the ring he turned the collet outwards and reappeared; he made several trials of the ring, and always with the same result —when he turned the collet inwards he became invisible, when outwards he reappeared. After this he contrived to be chosen one of the messengers who were sent to the court; where as soon as he arrived he seduced the queen, and with her help conspired against the king and slew him, and took the kingdom. Suppose now that there were two such magic rings, and the just put on one of them and the unjust the other; no man can be imagined to be of such an iron nature that he would stand fast in justice. No man would keep his hands off what was not his own when he could safely take what he liked out of the market, or go into houses and lie with any one at his pleasure, or kill or release from prison whom he would, and in all respects be like a God among men. Then the actions of the just would be as the actions of the unjust; they would both come at last to the same point. And this, we may truly affirm, is a convincing proof that men are just under compulsion and not willingly or because they think that justice is any good to them individually; for wherever any one thinks that he can safely be unjust, there he is unjust. All men believe in their hearts that injustice is far more profitable to the individual than justice. If you could imagine any one obtaining this power of becoming invisible, and never doing any wrong or touching what was another's, he would be thought by the lookers-on to be a miserable fool, although they would praise him to one another's faces, and keep up appearances with one another from a fear that they too might suffer injustice.

Now, if we are to form a real judgment of the life of the just and unjust, we must isolate them; there is no other way; and how is the isolation to be effected? I answer: Let the unjust man be entirely unjust, and the just man entirely just; nothing is to be taken away from either of them, and both are to be perfectly equipped for the work of their respective lives. First, let the unjust be like other distinguished masters of craft; like the skilful pilot or physician, who knows intuitively his own powers and keeps within their limits, and who, if he fails at any point, is able to recover himself. So let the unjust make his unjust attempts in the right way, and escape detection if he is to be a master of injustice: (criminals who are detected must be regarded as poor creatures): for the highest achievement of injustice is, to be thought just when you are not. So I say that in the perfectly unjust man we must assume the most perfect injustice; there is to be no deduction, but we must allow him, while doing the most unjust acts, to have acquired the greatest reputation for justice. If he have taken a false step he must be able to recover himself; he must be one who can speak with effect, if any of his acts come to light, and who can force his way where force is required by his courage and strength, and command of money and friends. And at his side let us place the just man in his nobleness and simplicity, wishing, as Aeschylus says, to be and not to seem good. There must be no seeming, for if he seem to be just he will be honoured and rewarded, and then we shall not know whether he is just for the sake of justice or for the sake of honours and rewards; he must be stripped of everything but justice; and he must be imagined in a condition the very opposite of his rival. Let him be the best of men, and let him be thought the worst; then he will have been put to the proof; and we shall see whether he will be affected by the fear of infamy and its consequences. And let him continue so to the hour of death; being just and seeming to be unjust. When both have reached the uttermost extreme, the one of justice and the other of injustice, let judgment be given which of them is the happier of the two.

Heavens! my dear Glaucon, I said, how energetically you polish them up for the decision, first one and then the other, as if they were two statues.

I do my best, he said. And now that we know what they are like there is no difficulty in tracing out the sort of life which awaits either of them. This I will proceed to describe. Let me put my words into the mouths of the eulogists of injustice. They will tell you that the just man who is thought unjust will be scourged, racked, bound—will have his eyes burnt out; and, at last, after suffering every kind of evil, he will be crucified. Then he will understand that he ought to seem only, and not to be, just; the words of Aeschylus may be more truly spoken of the unjust than of the just. For the unjust is pursuing a reality; he does not live with a view to appearances—he wants to be really unjust and not to seem only:—

> His mind has a soil deep and fertile,
> Out of which spring his prudent counsels.

In the first place, he is thought just, and so is among the rulers of the state: he can marry whom he likes, and give his children in marriage to whom he likes; also he can trade and deal where he wishes, and always to his own advantage, because he has no misgivings about injustice; and at every contest, whether in public or private, he gets the better of his antagonists, and gains at their expense, and is rich, and out of his gains he can benefit his friends, and harm his enemies; besides, he can offer sacrifices, and dedicate gifts to the gods abundantly and magnificently, and can honour the gods or any man whom he wants to honour in a far better style than the just, and so he is likely to be dearer than they are to the gods. Hence, Socrates, the saying that gods and men unite in making the life of the unjust better than the life of the just.[1]

Plato's reply is effectively given in a brief sentence, which contains the whole doctrine of natural morality. 'Goodness is the health and beauty and well-being of the soul, while evil is its disease, deformity and weakness.'[2] But the following passage contains a fuller answer.

Let us make an image[3] of the soul. Model the form of a many-headed monster, with a ring of heads of all kinds of beasts, tame and wild, which he can produce and change at will. Suppose now

[1] *Republic*, 359 f. [2] Ibid., 444.

[3] Ibid., 588 f. In this 'image' of human nature, man is three persons in one: the 'beast with many heads' is the complex of human appetites and desires; the 'lion' is the 'spirited', passionate, emotional, element, source of courage and energy and 'drive', which is in itself neutral and may be put at the service of a good or a bad cause, and appear either as the daemonic force of a Caesar Borgia, or as the heroism of a Joan of Arc; the 'man' is the rational element, immortal and divine. 'Injustice' is the enslavement of the 'man' to his desires or emotions; 'justice' is the harmony of desire and emotion under the control of reason.

that you make a second form of a lion, and a third of a man, the second smaller than the first, and the third smaller than the second. And now join them, and let the three grow into one. Next enclose them in the shape of a man so that any one unable to look inside would believe the creature to be a single human being. And now, when some one maintains that it is profitable for men to be unjust, and unprofitable to be just, let us reply that, if he be right, it is profitable for this creature to feast the many-headed monster and strengthen the lion and the lion-like qualities, but to starve and weaken the man, who is consequently liable to be dragged about at the mercy of either of the other two; and he is not to attempt to familiarize or harmonize them with one another—he ought rather to suffer them to fight and bite and devour one another.

Certainly, he said; that is what the advocate of injustice says.

And if we believe in justice we shall say that our words and actions should be such as to give the man within the most complete mastery over the entire human creature. He should watch over the many-headed monster like a good farmer, fostering and cultivating its tame elements, and preventing the wild ones from growing; he should be making the lion-heart his ally, and in common care of them all should reconcile the several parts with one another and with himself.

Come, now, and let us gently reason with the champion of injustice, whose error is unintentional. 'My dear friend,' we will say to him, 'what do you think, makes things noble or the reverse? Is it not the noble that which subjects the beast to the man, or rather to the god in man; and the ignoble that which subjects the man to the beast?' He can hardly avoid saying Yes. But, if he agree so far, we may ask him to answer another question: 'Then how would a man profit if he received gold and silver on the condition that he was to enslave the noblest part of him to the worst? Who can imagine that a man who sold his son or daughter into slavery for money, especially if he sold them into the hands of bad and cruel men, would be the gainer, however large might be the sum which he received? And if he enslaves without pity his own divine being to that which is most godless and detestable, is he not a wretched creature? Is not the age-old reproach of intemperance this—that it gives undue rein to that terrible, huge, multiform monster? And men are blamed for pride and bad temper when the element of the lion and serpent in them disproportionately grows and gains strength, and luxury and softness are blamed, because they relax and weaken the creature, and make a coward of him. Is not a man reproached for flattery and meanness who subordinates the spirited animal to the unruly monster, and, for the sake of money, of which he can never have enough, habituates him in the days of his youth to be trampled in the mire, and transforms him from a lion to a monkey? And so, as we are anxious to place man under a rule like that of the best, we say that he ought to be the servant of the best, in whom the Divine rules; not to the injury of the servant, but because every one had better be ruled by divine wisdom dwelling within him.

From what point of view, then, and on what ground can we say that it is in a man's interest to be unjust or intemperate or to do other disgraceful acts, which will make him a worse man, even though his wickedness brings him money or power? What shall he profit, if his injustice be undetected and unpunished? He who is undetected only gets worse, whereas he who is detected and punished has the brutal part of his nature silenced and humanized; the gentler element in him is liberated, and his whole soul is perfected and ennobled by the acquirement of justice and temperance and wisdom, more than the body ever is by beauty, strength, and health, inasmuch as the soul is more honourable than the body.

To this nobler purpose the man of understanding will devote the energies of his life. And in the first place, he will honour studies which impress these qualities on his soul, and will disregard others. In the next place, he will regulate his bodily habit and training, and so far will he be from yielding to brutal and irrational pleasures, that he will regard even health as quite a secondary matter; his first object will be not that he may be fair or strong or well, unless he is likely thereby to gain temperance, but he will always desire so to attemper the body as to preserve the harmony of the soul. And in the acquisition of wealth there is a principle of order and harmony which he will also observe; he will not allow himself to be dazzled by the foolish applause of the world, and amass wealth to his own infinite harm. He will look at the city of his soul, and watch that no disorder occur in it either from superfluity or from want of means; and upon this principle, so far as he can, he will regulate his property and gain or spend. For the same reason, he will gladly accept and enjoy such honours as he thinks likely to make him a better man; but those, whether private or public, which are likely to disorder his life, he will avoid. He will be a ruler in the city of which we are the founders, and which exists in idea only; for I do not believe that there is such an one anywhere on earth. In heaven there is laid up a pattern of it, which he who desires may behold, and beholding, may set his own house in order. But whether such city exists, or ever will exist in fact, is no matter; for he will live by its laws and by no others.

Ideals of Human Character and Life

The Laws *of Plato is an elaborate constitution for an imaginary state. Plato knew that most people obey laws mechanically and unintelligently, because the law is there and disobedience ends in the law court or the prison. So wishing to create in the citizens a spirit of intelligent and willing co-operation, he had the ingenious method of prefixing to his laws a 'preamble', which states the ultimate purposes and ideals that lie behind them. The following extract from such a preamble is interesting for the light which it throws on contemporary moral ideals.*

Of all the things which a man has, next to his gods, his soul is the most divine and most truly his own. Now in every man there are two parts: the better and superior, which rules, and the worse and inferior, which serves; and the ruling part of him is always to be preferred to the subject. So I am right in urging every one, next to the gods, who are our masters, to honour his own soul, which every one seems to honour, but no one honours as he ought; for honour is a divine good, and no evil thing is honourable; and he who thinks that he can honour the soul by word or gift, or any sort of compliance, without making her in any way better, seems to honour her, but honours her not at all. For example, every man, from his very boyhood, fancies that he is able to know everything, and thinks that he honours his soul by praising her, and is very ready to let her do whatever she may like. But my present contention is that in so acting he injures his soul, and is far from honouring her; whereas, in our opinion, he ought to honour her as second only to the gods. Again, when a man thinks that others are to be blamed, and not himself, for the errors which he has committed from time to time, and the many and great misfortunes which result, and always acquits himself as innocent, he is under the idea that he is honouring his soul; whereas the very reverse is the fact, for he is really injuring her. And when he indulges in pleasure in disobedience to the word and approval of the legislator, then again he is far from honouring her; he only dishonours her, and fills her full of evil and remorse; or when he does not endure to the end the labours and fears and sorrows and pains which the legislator approves, but gives way before them, then, by giving way, he does not honour the soul; conduct like this makes her dishonourable; nor when he thinks that life at any price is a good, does he honour her, but yet once more he dishonours her;

for the soul having a notion that the after world is all evil, he yields to her, and does not resist and teach or convince her that, for aught she knows, the world of the gods below, instead of being evil, may be the greatest of all goods. Again, when any one prefers beauty to virtue, what is this but the real and utter dishonour of the soul? For such a preference implies that the body is more honourable than the soul; and this is false, for there is nothing of earthly birth which is more honourable than the heavenly, and he who thinks otherwise of the soul has no idea how greatly he undervalues this wonderful possession. Nor again, when a man is eager to make money in dishonourable ways, and when he is not distressed by so making it, does he then honour his soul by such presents—far otherwise; he sells her glory and honour for a small piece of gold; but all the gold which is under or upon the earth is not enough to give in exchange for virtue. In a word, I may say that he who does not judge shame and evil, good and honour, by the standard of the legislator, and in every possible way avoid the one and practise the other to the utmost of his power, does not know that in all these respects he is most dishonourably and ignobly abusing his soul, which is the divinest part of man; for practically no one ever reflects on the greatest penalty of evil-doing—I mean, that we grow into the likeness of bad men, and, as we grow, shun the company of the good, and cut ourselves off from them, and cleave to and follow after the company of the bad. And he who is joined to them must do and suffer what such men by nature do and say to one another,—

a suffering which is not justice but retribution; for justice and the just are noble, whereas retribution is the suffering which waits upon injustice; and whether a man escape or endure this, he is miserable,—in the former case, because he is not cured; while in the latter, he perishes in order that the rest of mankind may be saved.

Speaking generally, our glory is to follow the better and improve the inferior, which is susceptible of improvement, as far as this is possible. And of all human possessions, the soul is by nature most inclined to avoid the evil, and track out and find the chief good; when a man has found it, he should take up his abode with it during the remainder of his life. So the soul is next to God in honour; and third, as every one will see, comes the honour of the body in natural order. Having determined this, we have next to consider that there is a natural honour of the body, and that of honours some are true and some are counterfeit. To decide which are which is the business of the legislator; and he, I suspect, would intimate that they are as follows: Honour is not to be given to the handsome body, or to the strong or the swift or the tall, or to the healthy body (although many may think otherwise), any more than to their opposites; but the intermediate states of all these habits are by far the safest and soundest; for the one extreme makes the soul braggart and insolent, and the other, illiberal and base; and money, and property, and distinction all go to the same tune. The excess of any of these things is apt to be a source of hatreds and divisions among states and individuals; and the defect of them is commonly a cause of slavery. And so I would not have any one fond of heaping up riches for the sake of his children, in order to leave them as rich as possible. The possession of great wealth is of no use, either to them or to the state. The condition of youth which is free from flattery, and at the same time not in need of the necessaries of life, is the best and most harmonious of all; it accords and agrees with our nature, and makes life most entirely free from sorrow. Let parents, then, bequeath to their children not riches but reverence (αἰδώς). We, indeed, fancy that they will inherit reverence from us, if we rebuke them when they show a want of it. But this quality is not really implanted in them by mere admonition. A sensible legislator will rather urge the old to reverence the young, and above all to take heed that no young man sees or hears one of themselves doing or saying anything disgraceful; for where the old have no shame, there the young will most certainly be devoid of it. The best way of training the young is to train yourself at the same time; not to preach, but always to practise what you would preach. He who honours his kindred, and respects those who share in the same gods and are of the same blood and family, may fairly expect the favour of the gods who preside over generation when he comes to found his family. And he who regards services which his friends and acquaintances do for him, as greater and more important than they themselves do, and his own favours to them less than theirs to him, will have their good-will in the intercourse of life. And surely in his relations to the state and his fellow-citizens, he is by far the best, who desires to win the palm of obedience to the laws of his country before any Olympic or any other victory of peace or war, and who, of all mankind, is the person reputed to have obeyed them best through life. In his relations to strangers, a man should consider that a contract is a most sacred thing, and that all concerns and wrongs of strangers are more directly dependent on the protection of God, than wrongs done to citizens; for the stranger, because he has no kindred or friends, is more to be pitied by gods and men.

Thus we have fairly described the proper attitude of a man to his parents, and himself, and his own affairs; and also to the state, and his friends, and relations, to his own countrymen, and to strangers. Our next task is to consider what should be the character of a man if he is to live honourably in those fields which are the concern not of law but of the educational force of praise and blame, that makes him more tractable and amenable to the laws which we intend to impose.

Truth is the beginning of every good thing, both to gods and men; and he who would be blessed and happy, should be from the first a partaker of truth, that he may live a true man as long as possible, for then he can be trusted; but he is not to be trusted who loves voluntary falsehood, and he who loves involuntary falsehood is a fool. Neither condition is enviable, for the untrustworthy and ignorant has no friend, and as time advances he becomes known, and lays up in store for himself isolation in crabbed age when life is on the wane: so that, whether his children or friends are alive or not, he is equally solitary.—Worthy of honour is he who does no injustice, and of more than twofold honour, if he not only does no injustice himself, but hinders others from doing any; the first may count as one man, the second is worth many men, because he informs the rulers of the injustice of others. And yet more highly to be esteemed is he who co-operates with the rulers in correcting the citizens as far as he can—he shall be proclaimed the great and perfect citizen, and bear away the palm of virtue. The same praise may be given about temperance and wisdom, and all other goods which may be imparted to others, as well as acquired by a man for himself; he who imparts them shall be honoured as the man of men, and he who is willing, yet is not able, may be allowed the second place; but he who is jealous and will not, if he can help, allow others in a friendly way to share in any good thing, is deserving of blame: the good, however, which he has, is not to be undervalued by us because it is possessed by him, but must be acquired by us also to the utmost of our power. Let us, then, all compete for the prize of virtue, but without envy. For the unenvious nature increases the greatness of states—he himself competes in the race, blasting the fair fame of no man; but the envious, who thinks that he ought to get the better by defaming others, is less energetic himself in the pursuit of true virtue, and disheartens his rivals by his unjust slanders of them. And so he makes the whole city to enter the arena untrained in the practice of virtue, and diminishes her glory as far as in him lies. Now every man should be courageous, but he should also be gentle. From the cruel, or hardly curable, or altogether incurable acts of injustice done to him by others, a man can only escape by fighting and defending himself and conquering, and by never ceasing to punish them; and no man who is not of a noble spirit is able to do this. As to the actions of those who do evil, but whose evil is curable, in the first place, let us remember that the unjust man is not unjust of his own free will. For no man of his own free will would choose to possess the greatest of evils, and least of all in his most precious part. And the soul, as we said, is in truth all men's most precious possession. In the soul, then, which is the most precious part of him, no one, if he could help, would admit, or allow to continue the greatest of evils. The unrighteous and vicious are always to be pitied in any case; and one can afford to forgive as well as pity him who is curable, and refrain and calm one's anger, not getting into a passion, like a woman, and nursing ill-feeling. But upon him who is incapable of reformation and wholly evil, the vials of our wrath should be poured out; so I say that good men ought, when occasion demands, to be both gentle and passionate.

Of all evils the greatest is one which is innate in the souls of most men, and which a man is always excusing in himself and never correcting; I mean, what is expressed in the saying that 'Every man by nature is and ought to be his own friend'. Whereas in all men the excessive love of self is in reality the source of all their wrong acts. If a man wishes to be great, he ought to regard, not himself or his interests, but justice, whether it is a question of his own or of others' acts. Through a similar error men are induced to fancy that their own ignorance is wisdom, and thus we who may be truly said to know nothing, think that we know all things; and because we will not let others act for us in what we do not know, we are compelled to act amiss ourselves. So let every man avoid too much self-love, and condescend to follow a better man than himself, and not allow any false shame to stand in the way. There are also minor precepts which are often repeated, and are quite as useful; a man should recollect them and remind himself of them. For when a stream is flowing out, there should be water flowing in too; and recollection repairs the waste of wisdom. So I say that a man should avoid excess either of laughter or tears, and should urge his neighbour to do the same; he should veil his immoderate sorrow or joy, and seek to behave with propriety, whether the genius of his good fortune remains with him, or whether at the crisis of his fate, when he seems to be mounting high and steep places, the gods oppose him in some of his enterprises. Still he may ever hope, in the case of good men, that whatever afflictions are to befall them in the future God will lessen, and that present evils He will change for the better; and as to the goods which are the opposite of these evils, he will not doubt that by heaven's blessing they will be his.[1]

The life which is thought happiest by the gods, is also the best.[2]

[1] *Laws*, 726 f.
[2] Ibid., 664.

The Rule of Reason

I see that the basis of human life lies in three wants and desires, which, if men are rightly guided, lead to virtue, if otherwise, to its opposite. The first two are eating and drinking, which begin at birth—every animal has a natural desire for them, and is violently excited, and rebels against anyone who says that he must not satisfy all his pleasures and appetites—and the third and greatest and sharpest want and desire breaks out last, and is sexual desire whose violent and wanton fires inflame men utterly with madness. These three disorders we must try to master by the three great principles of fear and law and right reason; turning them away from that which is called pleasantest to that which is best.[1]

Reason and Law

May we not conceive each of us living beings to be a puppet of the gods, either their plaything only, or created with a purpose—which of the two we cannot certainly know? But we do know, that these affections in us are like cords and strings, which pull us different and opposite ways, and to opposite actions; and herein lies the difference between virtue and vice. There is one among these cords which every man ought to grasp and never let go, but to pull with it against all the rest; and this is the sacred and golden cord of reason, called by us the common law of the State; there are others which are hard and of iron, but this one is soft because it is of gold; and there are several

[1] *Laws*, 782.

other kinds. Now we ought always to co-operate with the noblest guidance, which is that of law. For since reason is beautiful and gentle, and not violent, her guidance needs helpers to aid the golden principle in us to conquer the rest.[1]

Some Ideals

Indifference to Public Opinion

In questions of just and unjust, fair and foul, good and evil, which are the subjects of our present discussion, ought we to follow the opinion of the masses and to fear them; or the opinion of the one expert? ought we not to fear and respect him more than all the rest of the world: and if we desert him shall we not destroy and injure that principle in us which may be assumed to be improved by justice and deteriorated by injustice;—there is such a principle. And will life be worth having, if that higher part of man be destroyed, which is improved by right and depraved by wrong? Do we suppose that principle, whatever it may be in man, which has to do with justice and injustice, to be inferior to the body? If not, we must not regard what the crowd say of us: but what he, the one man who is an expert in right and wrong, will say, and what truth will say.[2]

The Fear of Death

A man who is good for anything ought not to calculate the chance of living or dying; he ought only to consider whether in doing anything he is doing right or wrong—acting the part of a good

[1] Ibid., 644 f. [2] *Crito*, 47 f.

man or of a bad. Whereas, upon your view, the heroes who fell at Troy were not good for much, and Achilles above all, who utterly despised danger in comparison with disgrace; and when he was so eager to kill Hector, his goddess mother said to him, that if he avenged his companion Patroclus, and slew Hector, he would die himself—'Fate,' she said, in these or the like words, 'waits for you next after Hector;' he, receiving this warning, utterly despised danger and death, and instead of fearing them, feared rather to live in dishonour, and not to avenge his friend. 'Let me die forthwith,' he replies, 'and be avenged of my enemy, rather than abide here by the beaked ships, a laughing-stock and a burden of the earth.' Had Achilles any thought of death and danger? Whereever a man's place is, whether the place which he has chosen or that in which he has been placed by a commander, there he ought to remain in the hour of danger; he should not think of death or of anything but of disgrace.[1]

The difficulty is not to avoid death, but to avoid unrighteousness; for that runs faster than death.[2]

Sexual Morals

A man is drawn different ways, and is in doubt between two principles; the one urging him to enjoy the beauty of youth, and the other forbidding him. For the one is a lover of the body, and hungers after beauty, like ripe fruit, and would fain satisfy himself without any regard to the character of his darling; the other, a soul that in

[1] *Apology*, 28. [2] Ibid., 39.

truth desires another soul, holds the desire of the body to be a secondary thing, looks rather than loves, and regards the satisfaction of physical love as wantonness; he reverences, yes and worships, temperance and courage and magnanimity and wisdom, and wishes to live in purity with the pure object of his affection.[1]

Our citizens ought not to fall below the level of birds and many other animals, which are born in great herds, and yet remain until the age for procreation virgin and unmarried, but when they have reached the proper time of life are coupled, male and female, and lovingly pair together, and live the rest of their lives in holiness and innocence, holding firmly to their original compact:—surely, we will say to them, you should be better than animals.[2]

The Duty of Marriage

A man should cling to immortality, and leave behind him children's children to be the servants of God in his place for ever. But if he will not listen, and remains unsocial and alien among his fellow-citizens, and is still unmarried at thirty-five years of age, let him pay a yearly fine.[3]

[1] *Laws*, 837.
[2] Ibid., 840.
[3] Ibid., 774.

CHAPTER VII

ART AND POETRY

Plato here raises the problem of the nature of poetry and of the influence exercised over the human mind, not only by poets but by actors, reciters, critics, and others who interpret poetry. He treats the question in a characteristic way, half playfully, half seriously. He is speaking to Ion, a rhapsode or professional reciter of poetry.

The gift which you possess of speaking excellently about Homer is not an art, but an inspiration; there is a divinity moving you, like that contained in a magnet. This stone not only attracts iron rings, but also imparts to them a similar power of attracting other rings; and sometimes you may see a number of pieces of iron and rings suspended from one another so as to form quite a long chain: and all of them derive their power of suspension from the original stone. Similarly the Muse first of all inspires men herself; and from these inspired persons is suspended a chain of other persons who take the inspiration. For all good poets, epic as well as lyric, compose their beautiful poems not by art, but because they are inspired and possessed. The lyric poets are not in their right mind when they are composing their fine strains: but they fall under the power of music and metre and are inspired and possessed; like the women who follow Bacchus and who draw milk and honey from the rivers when they are under his influence and not in their right mind.

And the soul of the lyric poet does the same, as they themselves say; for they tell us that they bring songs from honeyed fountains, culling them out of the gardens and dells of the Muses; they, like the bees, winging their way from flower to flower. And this is true. For the poet is a light and winged and holy thing, and he has no power of creation until he has been inspired and is out of his senses, and the mind is no longer in him: when he has not attained to this state, he is powerless and is unable to utter his oracles. Many are the noble words in which poets tell about the actions of men; but like yourself when speaking about Homer, they do not do it by any rules of art: they are simply inspired to utter that to which the Muse impels them, and that only; and when inspired, one of them will make dithyrambs, another hymns of praise, another choral strains, another epic or iambic verses—and he who is good at one is not good at any other kind of verse: for not by art does the poet sing, but by power divine. Had he learned by rules of art, he would have known how to speak not of one theme only, but of all; and so God takes away the minds of poets, and uses them as his ministers, as he also uses diviners and holy prophets, in order that we who hear them may know them to be speaking not of themselves who utter these priceless words in a state of unconsciousness, but that God himself is the speaker, and that through them he is talking with us.

I wish you would frankly answer, Ion, the question that I am going to ask you: When you produce the greatest effect upon the audience in the recitation of some striking passage, such as the apparition of Odysseus leaping forth on the floor, recognized by the suitors and casting his arrows at his feet, or the description of Achilles rushing at Hector, or the sorrows of Andromache, Hecuba, or Priam,—are you in your right mind? Are you not carried out of yourself, and does not your soul in an ecstasy seem to be among the persons or places of which you are speaking, whether they are in Ithaca or in Troy or whatever may be the scene of the poem?

Ion. That proof strikes home to me, Socrates. For I must frankly confess that at the tale of pity my eyes are filled with tears, and when I speak of horrors, my hair stands on end and my heart throbs.

Soc. Well, Ion, and what are we to say of a man who appears at a sacrifice or festival, dressed in holiday attire, with golden crowns upon his head, and bursts into tears, though he has lost none of his finery, or looks panic-stricken in the presence of more than twenty thousand friendly faces, when there is no one robbing or wronging him;—is he in his right mind or is he not?

Ion. No indeed, Socrates, I must say that, strictly speaking, he is not in his right mind.

Soc. And are you aware that you produce similar effects on most of the spectators?

Ion. Only too well; for I look down upon them from the stage, and behold the various emotions of pity, wonder, sternness, stamped upon their countenances when I am speaking: and I am obliged to give my very best attention to them;

for if I make them cry I myself shall laugh, and if I make them laugh I myself shall cry when the time of payment arrives.

Soc. Do you know that the spectator is the last of the rings which, as I am saying, receive the power of the original magnet from one another? The rhapsode like yourself and the actor are intermediate links, and the poet himself is the first of them. Through all these the God sways the souls of men in any direction which he pleases, and makes one man hang down from another. Thus there is a vast chain of dancers and masters and under-masters of choruses, who are suspended, as if from a magnet, at the side of the rings which hang down from the Muse.[1]

Art and Life

The passages that follow show Plato's genius for seeing and raising fundamental problems. Few people will agree with his ideal of State censorship; the results can be seen in Germany and Russia. But few, with the contrast between the films and the B.B.C., will be enthusiastic about the results of leaving everything to popular taste and financial interests. Perhaps the third extract suggests the right compromise, embodied in this country in the B.B.C.

(*a*) *The extravagances and dangers of new movements in art.*

As time went on, the poets themselves introduced the reign of vulgar and lawless innovation. They were men of genius, but they had no perception of what is legitimate in music; raging like

[1] *Ion*, 533 f.

Bacchanals and possessed with inordinate delights—mingling lamentations with hymns, and paeans with dithyrambs; imitating the sounds of the flute on the lyre, and making one general confusion; ignorantly affirming that music has no truth, and, whether good or bad, can only be judged of rightly by the pleasure which it gives to the hearer. And by composing such licentious works, and adding to them words as licentious, they have inspired the masses with lawlessness and boldness, and made them fancy that they can judge for themselves about melody and song. And in this way the audiences have found their tongues, as though they were expert judges of good and bad in music and poetry; and instead of an aristocracy, an evil sort of theatrocracy has grown up. If the democracy which judged had only consisted of educated persons, no fatal harm would have been done; but in music there first arose the universal conceit of omniscience and general lawlessness;—freedom came following afterwards, and men fancying that they knew what they did not know, lost all sense of fear; and the absence of fear begets shamelessness. That is just what this bad form of shamelessness is—an audacious refusal to respect the opinion of one's betters, due to a reckless form of liberty.[1]

(*b*) *State censorship: the extreme view.*

If any of the serious poets, as they are termed, who write tragedy, come to us and say—'Strangers, may we go to your city and country or may we not, and shall we bring with us our poetry—

[1] *Laws*, 700 f.

what is your will on this point?—how shall we answer these inspired men? I think that our answer should be as follows:—Best of strangers, we will say to them, we also according to our ability are tragic poets, and no tragedy is better or nobler than ours: for our whole state is framed to reproduce the highest and noblest life, and this we affirm to be indeed the very truth of tragedy. You are poets and we are poets, both makers of the same strains, rivals and antagonists in the noblest of dramas, which true law can alone perfect, as our hope is. Do not then suppose that we shall all in a moment allow you to erect your stage in the market place, or introduce the musical voices of your actors, speaking above our own, and permit you to harangue our women and children, and the common people, about our institutions, in language other than our own, and very often the opposite of our own.[1]

(*c*) *A* media via.

So far I too should agree with the popular view, that the excellence of music is to be measured by pleasure. But the pleasure must not be anybody's pleasure; the most beautiful music is that which delights the best and best educated natures, and especially that which delights the one man who is pre-eminent in virtue and education. And so the judges[2] must be men of character, for they will

[1] Ibid., 817.

[2] At the great festivals selected dramas were exhibited and judged by picked judges. Plato here and elsewhere comments on the unsatisfactory results in other Greek states where the decision was left to the audience.

require both wisdom and courage; the true judge must not draw his inspiration from the theatre, nor ought he to be unnerved by the clamour of the masses and his own incapacity. He is sitting not as the disciple of the theatre, but, in his proper place, as their instructor, and he ought to be the enemy of all pandering to the pleasure of the spectators. The ancient and common custom of Hellas, which still prevails in Italy and Sicily, did certainly leave the judgment to the body of spectators, who determined the victor by show of hands. But this custom has been the destruction of the poets; for they are now in the habit of composing with a view to please the bad taste of their judges, and the result is that the spectators instruct themselves;—and also it has been the ruin of the theatre; men ought to have characters put before them better than their own, and so receive a higher pleasure, but now by their own act the opposite result follows.[1]

[1] *Laws*, 659 f.

CHAPTER VIII

MISCELLANEOUS

The Intellectual Life

Truth is beautiful and enduring.[1]

Some things I have said of which I am not altogether confident. But that we shall be better and braver and less helpless if we think that we ought to enquire, than we should have been if we indulged in the idle fancy that there was no knowing and no use in seeking to know what we do not know;—that is a theme upon which I am ready to fight, in word and deed, to the utmost of my power.[2]

I am and always have been one of those natures who must be guided by reason, whatever the reason may be which upon reflection appears to me to be the best.[3]

Let us take care not to become misologists: no worse thing can happen to a man than this. For as there are misanthropists or haters of men, there are also misologists or haters of thought, and both spring from the same cause, which is ignorance of the world. Misanthropy arises out of the too great confidence of inexperience;—you trust a man and think him altogether true and sound and faithful, and then in a little while he turns out to be false

[1] *Laws*, 664. [2] *Meno*, 86. [3] *Crito*, 46.

and a rogue; and then another and another, and when this has happened several times to a man, especially when it happens among those whom he regarded as his own most trusted and familiar friends, and he has often quarrelled with them, he at last hates all men, and believes that no one has any good in him at all. But is not the feeling discreditable? Is it not obvious that such a person was trying to deal with men without any experience of human nature; for experience would have taught him the truth that there are few good men and few bad ones, and that the great majority are between the two. The point of my comparison is, that when a simple man who has no skill in dialectics believes an argument to be true which he afterwards imagines to be false, whether really false or not, and then another and another, he has no longer any faith left, and great disputers, as you know, come to think at last that they have grown to be the wisest of mankind; for they alone perceive the utter unsoundness and instability of all arguments, or indeed, of all things, which, like the currents in the Euripus, go up and down in never-ceasing ebb and flow. But how melancholy, if there be such a thing as truth or certainty or possibility of knowledge—that a man should have lighted upon some argument or other which at first seemed true and then turned out to be false, and instead of blaming himself and his own want of intelligence, because he is annoyed, should at last be too glad to transfer the blame from himself to arguments in general: and for ever afterwards should hate and abuse them, and lose truth and the knowledge of realities. Let us then be careful of allowing or of admitting into our souls the notion that there is no health or soundness in any arguments at all. Rather say that we have not yet attained to soundness in ourselves, and that we must struggle courageously and do our best to gain health of mind.[1]

I am one of those who are very willing to be corrected if I say anything which is not true, and very willing to correct any one else who says what is not true, and quite as ready to be corrected as to correct; for I hold that this is the greater gain of the two, just as the gain is greater of being cured of a very great evil than of curing another.[2]

The uncriticized life is not worth living.[3]

I seem to myself to see one very large and bad sort of ignorance which is quite distinct, and may be weighed in the scale against all other sorts of ignorance put together—when a person supposes that he knows, and does not know; this appears to be the great source of all the errors of the intellect.[4]

The noblest of all studies is the study of what man should be and what he should pursue.[5]

Those who have no natural aptitude for justice and other noble ideals, and no affinity with them, will never learn the full truth about good and evil, however good their intelligence and memory may be in other fields.[6]

[1] *Phaedo*, 89 f. [2] *Gorgias*, 458. [3] *Apology*, 38.
[4] *Sophist*, 229. [5] *Gorgias*, 487. [6] *Letters*, vii. 344.

The deepest truth cannot, like other objects of study, be put into words: from long intercourse and close intimacy with the facts, it comes suddenly into existence in the soul, like a light kindled by a flying spark, and at once becomes self-supporting.[1]

Two Kinds of Lie

The true lie, if such an expression may be allowed, is hated of gods and men. I mean that no one is willingly deceived in the truest and highest part of himself, or about the truest and highest matters; there, above all, he is most afraid of a lie having possession of him.

I do not understand you, he said.

The reason is, I replied, that you attribute some profound meaning to my words; but I am only saying that deception, or being deceived or uninformed about the highest realities in the highest part of themselves, which is the soul, and in that part of them to have and to hold the lie, is what mankind utterly detest. And, as I was just now remarking, this ignorance in the soul of him who is deceived may be called the true lie; for the lie in words is only a kind of imitation and shadowy image of a previous affection of the soul, not pure unadulterated falsehood. The true lie is hated not only by the gods, but also by men, whereas the lie in words is in certain cases useful and not hateful; in dealing with enemies—that would be an instance; or again, when those whom we call our friends in a fit of madness or illusion are going to do some harm, then it is useful and is a sort of

[1] *Letters*, vii. 241.

medicine or preventive; also in the tales of mythology, of which we were just now speaking—because we do not know the truth about ancient times, we make falsehood as much like truth as we can, and so turn it to account.[1]

Doctors and Judges

Both the passages that follow, though full of typically Platonic irony, are fundamentally serious.

The most skilful physicians are those who, from their youth upwards, have combined with the knowledge of their art the greatest experience of disease; they had better not be robust in health, and should themselves have suffered from all kinds of illnesses. For the body, as I conceive, is not the instrument with which they cure the body; in that case we could not allow them ever to be or to have been sickly; but they cure the body with the mind, and the mind which has become and is sick can cure nothing.

The judge is in a different position: he governs mind by mind; he ought not therefore to have been trained among vicious minds, and to have associated with them from youth upwards, and to have gone through the whole calendar of crime, only in order that he may quickly infer the crimes of others as he might their bodily diseases from his own self-consciousness; the honourable mind which is to form a healthy judgment should have had no experience or contamination of evil habits when young. And this is the reason why in youth good men often appear to be simple, and are easily

[1] *Republic*, 382.

practised upon by the dishonest, because they have no examples of what evil is in their own souls. So the judge should not be young; he should have learned to know evil, not from his own soul, but from late and long observation of the nature of evil in others: knowledge should be his guide, not personal experience. Further, he should be a good man. But the cunning and suspicious nature of which we spoke,—the man who has committed many crimes and fancies himself to be a master in wickedness, when in the company of people like himself, seems, with all his precautions, a clever fellow—he judges his companions by himself: but when he gets into the company of good men his misplaced suspicions make him seem silly; he cannot recognize an honest man, because he has no pattern of honesty in himself; at the same time, as the bad are more numerous than the good, and he meets with them oftener, he thinks himself, and is by others thought to be, rather wise than foolish. Not such is the good and wise judge for whom we are looking. He is the other type. For vice cannot know virtue too, but a virtuous nature, educated by time, will acquire a knowledge both of virtue and vice: the virtuous, and not the vicious man has wisdom—in my opinion.[1]

The use and abuse of medicine. An austere view of ill health.

To require the help of medicine, not when a wound has to be cured, or on occasion of an epidemic, but just because, by indolence and a

[1] *Republic*, 408 f.

self-indulgent habit of life, men fill themselves with waters and winds, as if their bodies were a marsh, compelling the ingenious sons of Asclepius[1] to find more names for diseases; is not this, too, a disgrace?

Yes, he said, they do certainly give very strange and new-fangled names to diseases.

Yes, I replied, and I do not believe that there were any such diseases in the days of Asclepius; and this I infer from the circumstance that the hero Eurypylus, after he has been wounded in Homer, drinks a posset of Pramnian wine well sprinkled with barley-meal and grated cheese, which are certainly inflammatory, and yet the sons of Asclepius who were at the Trojan war do not blame the woman who gives him the drink.

Well, he said, that was surely an extraordinary drink to be given to a person in his condition.

No so extraordinary, I replied, if you bear in mind that in former days, before the time of Herodicus, the guild of Asclepius did not practise our present system of medicine, which may be said to educate diseases. But Herodicus, who was a trainer, and himself of a sickly constitution, by a combination of training and doctoring found out a way of torturing first and chiefly himself, and secondly the rest of the world.

How was that? he said.

By the invention of lingering death; for he had a mortal disease which he perpetually nursed, and as recovery was out of the question, he passed his entire life as a valetudinarian; he could do nothing but attend upon himself, and he was in constant

[1] i.e. doctors. Asclepius is the god of healing.

torment whenever he made the least change in his usual regimen, and so dying hard, by the help of science he struggled on to old age.

A rare reward of his skill!

Yes, I said; a reward which a man might fairly expect who never understood that, if Asclepius did not instruct his descendants in this type of medicine, the omission arose, not from ignorance or inexperience of it, but because he knew that in all well-ordered states every individual has an occupation to which he must attend, and has therefore no leisure to spend in continually being ill. This we remark in the case of the artisan, but, ludicrously enough, do not apply the same rule to people of the richer sort.

How do you mean? he said.

I mean this: When a carpenter is ill he asks the doctor for a rough and ready cure; an emetic or a purge or a cautery or the knife,—these are his remedies. And if some one prescribes for him a course of dietetics, and tells him that he must swathe and swaddle his head, and all that sort of thing, he replies at once that he has no time to be ill, and that he sees no good in a life which is spent in nursing his disease to the neglect of his customary employment; and so bidding good-bye to this sort of physician, he resumes his ordinary habits, and either gets well and lives and does his business, or, if his constitution fails, he dies and has no more trouble.

Yes, he said, and a man in his condition of life ought to use the art of medicine so far only.

Has he not, I said, an occupation; and what profit would there be in his life if he were deprived of his occupation? But with the rich man it is otherwise; of him we do not say that he has any specially appointed work which he must perform, if he would live.

He is generally supposed to have nothing to do.

Then you never heard of the saying of Phocylides, that as soon as a man has a livelihood he should practise virtue?

I think, he said, that he had better begin rather sooner. Such excessive care of the body is most inimical to the practice of virtue, and equally incompatible with the management of a house, an army, or an office of state; and, what is most important of all, irreconcileable with any kind of study or thought or self-reflection—there is a constant suspicion that headache and giddiness are to be ascribed to philosophy, and accordingly all practising or making trial of virtue in the higher sense is absolutely stopped; for a man is always fancying that he is being made ill, and is in constant anxiety about the state of his body. And so our politic Asclepius may be supposed to have exhibited the power of his art only to persons who, being generally of healthy constitution and habits of life, had a definite ailment; such patients he cured by purges and operations, and told them to live normal lives, herein consulting the interests of the State; but bodies which disease had penetrated through and through he would not have attempted to cure: he did not want to lengthen out good-for-nothing lives, or to have weak fathers begetting weaker sons;—if a man was not able to live in the ordinary way he had no business to cure him; for such a cure would have been of no use either to the man, or to the State.

Then, he said, you regard Asclepius as a statesman.[1]

Two Types of Doctors

Did you ever observe that there are two classes of patients in states, slaves and freemen; and the slave-doctors run about and cure the slaves, or wait for them in the dispensaries—practitioners of this sort never talk to their patients individually, or let them talk about their own individual complaints? The slave-doctor prescribes what mere experience suggests, as if he had exact knowledge; and when he has given his orders, like a despot, he rushes off with equal assurance to some other servant who is ill; and so he relieves the master of the house of the care of his invalid slaves. But the other doctor, who is a freeman, attends and practises upon freemen; and he carries his enquiries far back, and goes into the nature of the disorder; he talks with the patient and with his friends, and is at once getting information from the sick man, and also instructing him as far as he is able, and he will not prescribe for him until he has first convinced him; at last, when he has brought the patient more and more under his persuasive influences and set him on the road to health, he attempts to effect a cure.[2]

How to treat Servants

The right treatment of slaves is to behave properly to them, and to do to them, if possible,

[1] *Republic*, 405. [2] *Laws*, 720.

even more justice than to those who are our equals; the man who naturally and genuinely reverences justice, and hates injustice, is revealed in his dealings with any class of men to whom he can easily be unjust.[1]

The following passage shows how inaccurate is the view that the Greeks 'had no sense of history'.

Do you think that you can reckon the time which has elapsed since cities first existed and men were citizens of them? It must be vast and incalculable? And have not thousands and thousands of cities come into being during this period and as many perished? And has not each of them had every form of government many times over, now growing larger, now smaller, and again improving or declining?[2]

Plato goes on to say that 'the arts were unknown for ten million years'—that is his estimate of the length of pre-history—and that not more than one or two thousand years have elapsed since the rise of civilization.

[1] Ibid., 777. [2] Ibid., 676.

CHAPTER IX

FABLES AND MYTHS

Socrates and Phaedrus talking in the noonday heat under a tree hear the cicadas.

Socrates. I believe that the grasshoppers chirruping after their manner in the heat of the sun over our heads are talking to one another and looking down at us. What would they say if they saw that we, like the crowd, are not conversing, but slumbering at mid-day, lulled by their voices, too indolent to think? Would they not have a right to laugh at us? They might imagine that we were slaves, who come to rest at a place of resort of theirs, and like sheep lie asleep at noon around the well. But if they see us discussing, and sailing past them, deaf like Odysseus to their siren voices, they may perhaps, out of respect, give us of the gifts which the gods give them to impart to men.

Phaedrus. What gifts do you mean? I never heard of any.

Soc. A lover of music like yourself ought surely to have heard the story of the grasshoppers, who are said to have been human beings in an age before the Muses. And when the Muses came and poetry was born, they were ravished with delight; and singing always, never thought of eating and drinking, until at last in their forgetfulness they died. And now they live again in the grasshoppers; and this is the return which the Muses make to them—they neither hunger, nor thirst, but from the hour of their birth are always singing, and never eat or drink; and when they die they go and tell the Muses in heaven who honours them on earth.[1]

The Drawbacks of Books

Soc. At the Egyptian city of Naucratis, there was a famous old god, whose name was Theuth; the bird which is called the Ibis is sacred to him, and he was the inventor of many arts, such as arithmetic and calculation and geometry and astronomy and draughts and dice, but his great discovery was the use of letters. Now in those days the god Thamus was the king of the whole country of Egypt; and he lived in that great city of Upper Egypt which the Greeks call Egyptian Thebes. To him came Theuth and showed his inventions, desiring that the other Egyptians might be allowed to have the benefit of them; he enumerated them, and Thamus enquired about their several uses, and praised some of them and found fault with others, as he approved or disapproved of them. It would take a long time to repeat all that Thamus said to Theuth in praise or blame of the various arts. But when they came to letters, This, said Theuth, will make the Egyptians wiser and give them better memories; it is a specific both for the memory and for the wit. Thamus replied: Most ingenious Theuth, the parent or inventor of an art is not always the best judge of the utility or inutility of his own inventions to the users of them. And in this instance, you who are the father of letters, from a paternal love of your

[1] *Phaedrus*, 259.

own children, have been led to attribute to them a quality which they cannot have; for this discovery of yours will create forgetfulness in the learner's souls, because they will not use their memories; they will trust to the external written characters and not remember of themselves. The specific which you have discovered is an aid not to memory but to recollection, and you give your disciples not truth, but only the semblance of truth; they will hear much and learn nothing; they will appear to know much and will generally know nothing; they will be tiresome company, for they will seem wise without being wise.

Phaedr. Yes, Socrates, you have no difficulty in inventing tales of Egypt, or of any other country.[1]

The so-called 'myth' (of which two have been already quoted, pp. 53, 103.) is more than a fable or even than an allegory. Plato uses it to convey ideas which are matters for faith rather than reason, and may be believed but cannot be proved. Hence the myths generally end the dialogues—imaginative vision supplying an element which mere reasoning could not give. They 'burst in upon the Dialogue with a revelation of something new and strange: the narrow, matter-of-fact, workaday experience, which the argumentative conversation puts in evidence, is suddenly flooded and transfused by the inrush of a vast experience as from another world'.[2] Plato never claims exact truth for his myths: as he says, 'a

[1] *Phaedrus*, 274 f.
[2] Stewart, *Myths of Plato*, p. 2.

sensible man ought not insist on the accuracy of my details: but that this or something like it is the truth about our souls and their habitations, since the soul has been shown to be immortal—this seems to me a fitting belief and one worth venturing'.[1]

The following myths are 'eschatological'. The first is a vision of the last judgment and deals with evil and punishment.

Zeus and Poseidon and Pluto divided the empire which they inherited from their father. Now in the days of Cronos there existed a law that the man, who has lived all his life in justice and holiness shall go, when he is dead, to the Islands of the Blessed, and live there in perfect happiness out of the reach of evil; but that he whose life has been unjust and irreligious shall go to the house of vengeance and punishment, which is called Tartarus. And in the time of Cronos, and even quite lately in the reign of Zeus, the judgment was given on the very day on which the men were to die; the judges were alive, and the men were alive; and the consequence was that the judgments were unsatisfactory. Then Pluto and the authorities from the Islands of the Blessed came to Zeus, and said that the souls found their way to the wrong places. Zeus said: 'I shall put a stop to this; the judgments are bad, because the persons who are judged have their clothes on, for they are alive; and there are many who, having evil souls, are dressed in beautiful bodies, or encased in wealth or rank, and, when the day of judgment arrives, numerous witnesses come forward and

[1] *Phaedo*, 114.

testify on their behalf that they have lived righteously. The judges are awed by them, and they themselves too have their clothes on when judging; their eyes and ears and their whole bodies are interposed as a veil before their own souls. All this is a hindrance to them; there are the clothes of the judges and the clothes of the judged.—What is to be done? I will tell you:—In the first place, I will deprive men of the foreknowledge of death, which they possess at present: this power which they have Prometheus has already received my orders to take from them: in the second place, they shall be entirely stripped before they are judged, for they shall be judged when they are dead; and the judge too shall be naked, that is to say, dead—he with his naked soul shall see the other naked souls; and they shall die suddenly and be deprived of all their kindred, and leave their brave attire strewn upon the earth—conducted in this manner, the judgment will be just. I knew all about the matter before any of you, and therefore I have made my sons judges; two from Asia, Minos and Rhadamanthus, and one from Europe, Aeacus. And these, when they are dead, shall give judgment in the meadow at the parting of the ways, whence the two roads lead, one to the Islands of the Blessed, and the other to Tartarus. Rhadamanthus shall judge those who come from Asia, and Aeacus those who come from Europe. From this tale, Callicles, which I have heard and believe, I draw the following inferences:—Death, if I am right, is in the first place the separation from one another of two things, soul and body; nothing else. And after they are separated they retain their several natures, as in life; the body keeps the same habit, and the results of treatment or accident are distinctly visible in it: for example, he who by nature or training or both, was tall while he was alive, will remain as he was, after he is dead; and the fat man will remain fat; and so on; and the dead man, whose habit in life was to wear his hair long, will have long hair. And if he was marked with the whip and had the prints of the scourge, or of wounds in him when he was alive, you will see the same in the dead body; and if his limbs were broken or misshapen when he was alive, the same appearance would be visible in the dead. And in a word, whatever was the habit of the body during life would be distinguishable after death, either perfectly, or in a great measure and for a certain time. And I should imagine that this is equally true of the soul, Callicles; when a man is stripped of the body, all the natural or acquired affections of the soul are laid open to view.—And when they come to the judge, as those from Asia come to Rhadamanthus, he places them near him and inspects them quite impartially, not knowing whose the soul is: perhaps he may lay hands on the soul of the King of Persia, or of some other king or potentate, who has no soundness in him, but his soul is marked with the whip, and is full of the prints and scars of perjuries and crimes with which his various acts have stained him, and he is all crooked with falsehood and imposture, and has no straightness, because he has lived without truth. Him Rhadamanthus beholds, full of all deformity and disproportion, which is caused by licence and luxury and insolence and incontinence, and despatches him ignominiously to his prison, and there he undergoes the punishment which he deserves. Now punishment has a double function: a man who is rightly punished ought either to profit by it and improve, or he ought to become an example to others, that they may see what he suffers, and fear and become better. Those who are improved when they are punished by gods and men, are those whose sins are curable; and they are improved, as in this world so also in another, by pain and suffering; for there is no other way in which they can be delivered from their evil. But they who have been guilty of the worst crimes, and whose crimes are such that they are incurable, are made examples; for, as they are incurable, nothing can help them. They get no good themselves, but others get good when they see them enduring eternally the most terrible and painful and fearful sufferings as the penalty of their sins—there they are, hanging up as examples, in the prison-houses of the world below, a spectacle and a warning to all wicked men who come there. Of these fearful examples, most, as I believe, are taken from the class of despots and kings and potentates and public men, for they are the authors of the greatest and most impious crimes, because they have the power. The very bad men come from the class of those who have power. And yet good men may appear in that class and they deserve our warm admiration, for where there is great power to do wrong, it is difficult and praiseworthy to live a just life, and few achieve it. Such good and true men, however, there have been, and will be again, at Athens and in other states, who have fulfilled their trust righteously. But, in general, power and evil go together, my friend. As I was saying, Rhadamanthus, when he gets a soul of the bad kind, knows nothing about him, neither who he is, nor who his parents are; he knows only that he has got hold of a villain; and seeing this, he stamps him as curable or incurable, and sends him away to Tartarus, where he goes and receives his proper recompense. Or, again, he looks with admiration on the soul of some just one who has lived in holiness and truth; he may have been a private man or not; and I should say, Callicles, that he is most likely to have been a philosopher who has done his own work, and not troubled himself with the doings of other men in his lifetime; him Rhadamanthus sends to the Islands of the Blessed. Now I, Callicles, am persuaded of the truth of these things, and I consider how I shall present my soul whole and undefiled before the judge in that day. Renouncing the honours at which the world aims, I desire only to know the truth, and to live as well as I can, and, when I die, to die as well as I can. And, to the utmost of my power, I exhort all other men to do the same.[1]

The following myth deals with the destiny of the soul, with punishment and free will. Like the previous myth, it is coloured by Orphic ideas. The Orphics believed in the immortality and transmigration of the soul, holding that after death each soul was rewarded or punished ten times over for its deeds in the body and then was born again, unless the greatness of its virtues had earned heaven

[1] *Gorgias*, 523 f.

or the blackness of the crimes condemned it to eternal punishment.

I will tell you a tale of a hero, Er the son of Armenius, a Pamphylian by birth. He was killed in battle, and ten days afterwards, when the bodies of the dead were taken up already in a state of decay, his body was found unaffected, and carried away home to be buried. And on the twelfth day, as he was lying on the funeral pile, he returned to life and told them what he had seen in the other world. He said that when his soul left the body he went on a journey with a great company, and that they came to a mysterious place at which there were two openings in the earth; they were near together, and opposite them were two other openings in the heaven above. In the intermediate space there were judges seated, who directed the good, after they had given judgment on them and fastened their sentences in front of them, to ascend by the heavenly way on the right hand; and similarly the wicked were ordered by them to descend by the lower way on the left hand; these also bore the symbols of their deeds, but fastened on their backs. He drew near, and they told him that he was to take news of the other world to men, and they told him to hear and see all that was to be heard and seen in that place. Then he looked and saw on one side the souls leaving by the two openings of heaven and earth when sentence had been passed: and at the other two openings other souls, some ascending out of the earth dusty and worn with travel, some descending out of heaven clean and bright. And as they kept arriving they seemed to have come from a long journey, and they went forth with gladness into the meadow, where they encamped as at a festival; and those who knew one another embraced and conversed, the souls which came from earth curiously enquiring about the things above, and the souls which came from heaven about the things beneath. And they told one another of what had happened by the way, those from below weeping and sorrowing at the remembrance of the things which they had endured and seen in their journey beneath the earth (now the journey lasted a thousand years), while those from above were describing heavenly delights and visions of inconceivable beauty. The story, Glaucon, would take too long to tell; but the sum was this:—He said that for every wrong which they had done to any one they suffered tenfold; or once in a hundred years—such being reckoned to be the length of man's life, and the penalty being thus paid ten times in a thousand years. If, for example, there were any who had been the cause of many deaths, or had betrayed or enslaved cities or armies, or been partly responsible for any other villainy, for every one of their offences they were punished ten times over, and the rewards of beneficence and justice and holiness were in the same proportion. For piety and impiety to gods and parents, and for murder, there were even greater punishments which he described. He mentioned that he was present when one of the spirits asked another, 'Where is Ardiaeus the Great?' (Now this Ardiaeus lived a thousand years before the time of Er: he had been the prince of some city of Pamphylia, and had murdered his old father and his elder brother, and was said to have committed many other abominable crimes.) The answer of the other spirit was: 'He comes not hither and will never come. And this,' said he, 'was one of the dreadful sights which we ourselves witnessed. After all these experiences, as we were at the mouth of the cavern, and about to reascend, suddenly Ardiaeus appeared and several others, most of whom were despots; and there were also besides them private individuals who had been great criminals: they were just, as they fancied, about to return into the upper world, but the mouth, instead of admitting them, gave a roar, whenever any of these incurable sinners or some one who had not been sufficiently punished tried to ascend; and then wild men of fiery aspect, who were standing by and heard the sound, seized and carried them off; and Ardiaeus and others they bound head and foot and hand, and threw them down and flayed them with scourges, and dragged them along the road at the side, carding them on thorns like wool, and declaring to the passers-by what were their crimes, and that they were being taken away to be cast into hell.' And of all the many terrors which they had endured, he said that there was none like the terror which each of them felt at that moment, lest they should hear the voice; and when there was silence, one by one they ascended with great joy. These, said Er, were the penalties and retributions, and there were blessings as great.[1]

After seven days the spirits journey to a place where are the three Fates—Lachesis, Clotho, and Atropos.

[1] *Republic*, 614 f.

When Er and the spirits arrived, their duty was to go at once to Lachesis; but first of all there came an Interpreter who arranged them in order; then he took from the knees of Lachesis lots and samples of lives, and mounting a high pulpit, spoke as follows: 'Hear the word of Lachesis, the daughter of Necessity. Souls, beings of a day, behold a new cycle of life and mortality. Your destiny will not be allotted to you, but you will choose it; and let him who draws the first lot have the first choice, and the life which he chooses shall be his destiny. Virtue is free, and as a man honours or dishonours her he will have more or less of her; the responsibility is with the chooser—God is not responsible.' When the Interpreter had so spoken he scattered lots at random among them all, and each of them took up the lot which fell near him, all but Er himself (he was not allowed), and each as he took his lot saw the number which had fallen to him. Then the Interpreter placed on the ground before them samples of lives; and there were many more lives than the souls present, and they were of all sorts. There were lives of every animal and of man in every condition. And there were despotisms among them, some lasting out the despot's life, others which broke off in the middle and came to an end in poverty and exile and beggary; and there were lives of famous men, some who were famous for their personal beauty as well as for their strength and success in games, or, again, for their birth and the qualities of their ancestors; and some who were the reverse of famous for the opposite qualities. And so too with women. There was not, however, any definite character in them, because the soul must needs change, when it chooses a new life. But there was every other quality, and they were all mixed up with one another, and also with elements of wealth and poverty, and disease and health; and there were intermediate states also. Here, my dear Glaucon, is the supreme peril of our human state. So let each one of us, to the neglect of any other study, take every care to go in search and pursuit of that science, by which he may somehow learn and discover some one who will give him the power and knowledge and the gift of distinguishing between good and evil, and so make him able to choose always and everywhere the better life as he has opportunity. He should consider the bearing of all these qualities which have been mentioned severally and collectively upon virtue; he should know the effect of beauty combined with poverty or wealth in a particular soul, and the good and evil consequences of noble and humble birth, of private and public station, of strength and weakness, of cleverness and dullness, and of all the natural and acquired gifts of the soul, and the operation of them when conjoined; he will then look at the nature of the soul, and from the consideration of all these qualities he will be able to determine which is the better and which is the worse; and so he will choose, calling a life evil if it will make his soul more unjust, and good if it will make his soul more just; all else he will disregard. For we have seen and know that this is the best choice both in life and after death. A man must take with him into the world below an adamantine faith in truth and right, that there too he may be undazzled by the desire of wealth or the other attractions of evil, lest, coming upon despotisms and similar villainies, he do irremediable wrongs to others and suffer yet worse himself; but let him know how to choose the mean and avoid the extremes on either side, as far as possible, not only in this life but in all that which is to come. For this is the way of happiness. And according to the report of the messenger from the other world this was what the Interpreter said at the time: 'Even for the last comer, if he chooses wisely and will live strenuously, there is appointed a happy and not undesirable existence. Let not him who chooses first be careless, and let not the last despair.' When he had spoken, he who had the first choice came forward and in a moment chose the greatest despotism; in his thoughtlessness and greed, he had not considered everything before he chose, and did not at first sight observe that he was fated, among other evils, to devour his own children. But when he had time to reflect, and saw what was in the lot, he began to beat his breast and lament his choice, forgetting the proclamation of the Interpreter; instead of throwing the blame of his misfortune on himself, he accused chance and the gods, and everything rather than himself. He was one of those who came from heaven, and in a former life had dwelt in a well-ordered State, and his virtue was a mere habit, with no principle behind it. And it was true of others who were similarly overtaken, that the greater number of them came from heaven and therefore they had never been schooled by trial, whereas the pilgrims who came from earth having themselves suffered and seen others suffer were not in a hurry to choose. And owing to this inexperience of theirs, and also because the lot was a chance, many of the souls exchanged a good destiny for a bad one or a bad one for a good. For if a man had always on his arrival in this world dedicated himself from the first to sound philosophy, and had been moderately fortunate in the number of the lot, he might, as Er reported, be happy here, and also his journey to another life and return to this, instead of being rough and underground, would be smooth and heavenly. Most curious, he said, was the spectacle—sad and laughable and strange; for the choice of the souls was in most cases based on their experience of a previous life. There he saw the soul which had once been Orpheus[1] choosing the life of a swan from his hatred of the female sex: he would not be born of a woman because they had been his murderers; he beheld also the soul of Thamyras choosing the life of a nightingale; birds, on the other hand, like the swan and other songsters, wanting to be men. The soul which obtained the twentieth lot chose the life of a lion, and this was the soul of Ajax the son of Telamon, who would not be a man, remembering the injustice which was done him in the judgment about the arms. The next was Agamemnon, who took the life of an eagle, because, like Ajax, his sufferings had made

[1] Orpheus, refusing to marry after his wife's death, was killed by the women of Thrace. Thamyras, a legendary poet. Ajax failed to obtain the arms of Achilles, which after their owner's death were to be given to the bravest Greek. Epeus made the wooden horse by which the Greeks took Troy. For Thersites see *Troilus and Cressida*.

him hate human nature. About the middle came the lot of Atalanta; she, seeing the great fame of an athlete, was unable to resist the temptation: and after her there followed the soul of Epeus the son of Panopeus passing into the nature of a skilful craftswoman; and far away among the last who chose, the soul of the jester Thersites was putting on the form of a monkey. There came also the soul of Odysseus having yet to make a choice, and his lot happened to be the last of them all. Now the recollection of former toils had disenchanted him of ambition, and he went about for a considerable time in search of the life of a private man who had no cares; he had some difficulty in finding this; it was lying neglected by everybody else; and when he saw it, he said that he would have done the same had his lot been first instead of last, and that he was delighted to have it. And not only did men pass into animals, but I must also mention that there were animals tame and wild who changed into one another and into corresponding human natures—the good into the gentle and the evil into the savage, in all sorts of combinations. All the souls had now chosen their lives, and they went in the order of their choice to Lachesis,[1] who sent with them the Destiny whom they had severally chosen, to be the guardian of their lives and the fulfiller of their choice: this spirit led the souls first to Clotho, and drew them within the revolution of the spindle impelled by her hand, thus ratifying the destiny of each; and then, when they were fastened to this, carried them to Atropos,

[1] Lachesis allotted, Clotho spun, Atropos made irrevocable, the thread of life.

who spun the threads and made them irreversible. Thence without turning round they passed beneath the throne of Necessity; and when they had all passed, they marched on in a scorching heat to the plain of Forgetfulness, which was a barren waste destitute of trees and all vegetation; and then towards evening they encamped by the river of Forgetfulness, whose water no vessel can hold; of this they were all obliged to drink a certain quantity, and those who were not saved by wisdom drank more than was needful; and each one as he drank forgot all things. Now after they had gone to rest, about the middle of the night there was a thunderstorm and earthquake, and then in an instant they were driven upwards in all manner of ways to their birth, like stars shooting. He himself was hindered from drinking the water. But in what manner or by what means he returned to the body he could not say; only, in the morning, awaking suddenly, he found himself lying on the pyre. And thus, Glaucon, the tale has been saved and was not lost; and it will save us if we listen to it; and we shall pass safely over the river of Forgetfulness and our soul will not be defiled. So my counsel is, that we hold fast ever to the heavenly way and follow after justice and virtue always, considering that the soul is immortal and able to endure every sort of good and every sort of evil. Thus shall we live dear to one another and to the gods, both while remaining here and when we receive our reward. And it shall be well with us both in this life and in the pilgrimage of a thousand years which we have been describing.[1]

1 *Republic* 617 f.